Janelle Ho and
Helen Pearson

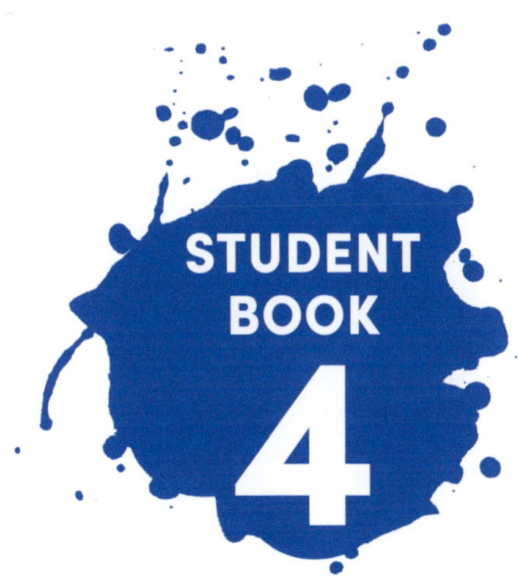

NSW Edition

Name: ______________________________

Class: ______________________________

Contents

SLLURP

SLLURP summarises the spelling strategies that you can use to learn new words.

Say	Say the word carefully and slowly to yourself.
Listen	Listen to how each part of the word sounds in sequence.
Look	Look at the patterns of letters in the word and the shape of the word.
Understand	Understand rules, word meanings and word origins.
Remember	Remember all the similar words you can already spell and relate this knowledge to any new word.
Practise	Practise writing the word until it is firmly fixed in your long-term memory.

Scope and Sequence

Unit	Vowels	Consonants	Letter patterns	Morphology and etymology	Homophones/ Confusing words	Topic words	WORD LIST
	SKILL FOCUS						
1	two-syllable words with long sounds, silent e			-s, -es, -ed, -ing: dropping silent e			oppose, endure, revise, complete, arrange, escape, persuade, realise, collide, assume, include, declare
2	short and long y		ay, ey, oy	-s, -es, -ed, -ing: changing y to i	pray/prey		copy, hurry, guilty, mystery, variety, deny, apply, simplify, qualify, display, prey, annoy
3				adding -ed, -ing to two-syllable words: doubling final consonant			begin, forget, regret, occur, prefer, enter, offer, visit, happen, target, label, detail
4		words ending in lf	ph, gh	phobia			engulf, behalf, cough, trough, phase, phobia, phantom, metaphor, emphasise, biography, amphibian, sophisticated
5		words ending in double consonants		-er, -est			odd, stiff, err, recall, install, swell, thrill, floss, discuss, possess, witness, embarrass
6	REVISION						
7	ea				led/lead, weather/ whether		least, eager, release, dread, ahead, heavy, health, meant, instead, pleasant, jealous, weather
8		soft g					ginger, gently, general, average, generous, religion, intelligent, fragile, generation, advantage, emergency, gymnasium
9		j	ge, dge, dj				bandage, sponge, surge, stranger, siege, badger, pledge, reject, injection, adjust, conjunction, adjective
10	ie, ei				rain/rein/reign		niece, belief, achieve, alien, receipt, deceive, protein, weird, reign, seize, beige, feisty
11					confusing pairs		lose, loose, breath, breathe, desert, dessert, practise, practice, wonder, wander, stationery, stationary
12	REVISION						
13	oa, ou		ow		fowl/foul		narrow, sorrow, tomorrow, loan, poach, coward, foul, announce, voucher, boundary, council, knowledge
14			er, ear				verse, superb, alert, convert, deserve, determined, certain, permanent, earthquake, research, earnest, rehearsal
15			or, ur, our	court-			worthy, senior, surprise, further, burden, survive, journal, flavour, labour, courtesy, honour, harbour
16			words ending in ure	thermo-, -meter			nature, future, capture, failure, creature, feature, measure, pleasure, leisure, adventure, furniture, temperature
17						colours, similes	ruby, scarlet, lilac, violet, emerald, indigo, crimson, azure, khaki, ochre, turquoise, sapphire
18	REVISION						
19			ex				exist, exchange, examination, explosion, expensive, exaggerate, excursion, exceed, except, extinct, exhausted, exhibition
20				un-, in-, dis-; *videre*			unfamiliar, undeveloped, unbroken, unquestioning, inactive, incomplete, informal, invisible, disease, disqualify, discontented, discontinue
21				-ion, -ness; *claudere*			rejection, suggestion, location, separation, confusion, decision, conclusion, greatness, selfishness, stubbornness, cleanliness, forgetfulness
22				-th	fourth/forth	ordinal numbers	fourth, fifth, eighth, ninth, twelfth, growth, warmth, length, strength, width, depth, breadth
23		double consonants			accept/except, affect/effect		accept, appeal, stubborn, villain, pollute, approach, opportunity, attitude, necessary, recommend, occasion, aggressive
24	REVISION						
25				-or, -er, -ant, -ian, -ist; apostrophes		occupations; non-English words	author, grocer, carpenter, lawyer, assistant, accountant, electrician, politician, journalist, pharmacist, chef, pilot
26			words ending in ous	-ous; rules for adding -ous			serious, precious, delicious, famous, nervous, dangerous, courageous, furious, cautious, envious, spacious, various
27				-ment			investment, accomplishment, assessment, disappointment, announcement, judgement, arrangement, agreement, enrolment, involvement, retirement, requirement
28				-ible, -able, -ly	illegible/eligible		affordable, enjoyable, renewable, agreeable, forgivable, recognisable, sociable, impossible, eligible, illegible, edible, audible
29				compound words; abbreviations		computers	computer, laptop, email, internet, mobile, keyboard, program, download, insert, delete, icon, archive
30	REVISION						
31				-ic; -ed, -ing; adding k			mimic, critic, exotic, acidic, dramatic, fantastic, terrific, tragic, energetic, automatic, enthusiastic, genetic
32			words ending in al	-al, il-, un-			capital, hospital, logical, magical, national, natural, digital, optical, criminal, critical, survival, emotional
33				-en, -ise: rules for adding -en, ise; *memor*			lessen, stiffen, toughen, sadden, awaken, straighten, finalise, memorise, fantasise, energise, sympathise, visualise
34						holidays	travel, relax, journey, caravan, luggage, budget, museum, attraction, entertainment, accommodation, sightseeing, restaurant
35	REVISION						

Note to Teachers and Parents

Spelling Rules!

Some students are natural spellers, but the vast majority of students need formal, systematic and sequential instruction about the way spelling works and the strategies they can use to become independent, confident spellers.

The *Spelling Rules!* program is based on sound linguistic and pedagogical theory. It is informed by research into how students of different ages acquire and apply spelling skills, and how those skills move from the working to the long-term memory. The program closely follows the NSW English Syllabus. NSW Syllabus references are provided in the two Teacher Resource Books. The program consists of seven Student Books.

Each student book contains units of work, with each unit designed to be used over the course of a week. The content of each unit follows the suggested instructional sequence in the NSW English Syllabus. Each unit simultaneously develops new skills and reinforces skills from previous units. Where appropriate, topic words from other syllabus areas are included. When spelling rules and tips are introduced, only known sounds and letter patterns are used so that students focus on one skill at a time. Regular revision units enable teachers to assess student progress and reinforce key rules and patterns from previous units. Books 1 to 4 also include a simple reflection activity that encourages students to assess their own progress and provides you with a starting point for discussion.

Spelling knowledge

Learning to spell involves developing different kinds of spelling knowledge:

- **Kinaesthetic knowledge** – the physical feeling when saying different sounds and words, and when writing the shapes of letters and words
- **Phonological knowledge** – how a word sounds and the patterns of sounds in words
- **Visual knowledge** – how letters and words look and the visual patterns in words
- **Morphemic knowledge** – the meaning or function of words or parts of words
- **Etymological knowledge** – the origins and history of words and the effect this has on spelling patterns.

Icons used in Student Book 4

The following icons identify the main spelling strategy that students will use to complete an activity.

Say the word. (Kinaesthetic knowledge) These activities ask students to experience how sounds feel in the mouth and jaw. Changing the positions of the jaw, lips and tongue changes the sounds we make. Encourage students to pronounce the sounds and words accurately. If they mispronounce a sound or word, they may misrepresent it in writing.

Listen to the word. (Phonological knowledge) These activities focus on discriminating between different sounds and breaking up words into syllables or individual sound segments (phonemes).

Look at the word. (Visual knowledge) These activities help students to see how the sound is represented using combinations of letters, and to associate this visual pattern with what they are hearing. Students will develop the ability to know when a word does or does not 'look right'.

Understand the word. (Morphemic and etymological knowledge) These activities focus on word meanings, word families, prefixes and suffixes, spelling rules, word origins and so on, which help embed spelling in the long-term memory.

Practise writing the word. (Kinaesthetic knowledge) These activities develop students' awareness of the physical movement involved in writing the word. By practising writing the word a number of times and in different contexts, the spelling becomes embedded in the long-term memory.

This icon highlights useful spelling rules.

This icon tells students that a special clue or hint is provided for an activity. It may be a spelling, grammar or punctuation convention, or a definition of a useful term.

The reflection encourages students to assess their progress across each unit.

Student Book 4

Units of work

Student Book 4 contains 35 weekly units of work. See the **Scope and Sequence chart** on page 3 for more information. Each revision unit gives students an opportunity to self-assess.

Word lists

In *Student Book 4*, each unit (except Revision) has a list of spelling words. The core words in the lists have been chosen to support the learning focus and strategies being taught in the unit.

Spelling lists enable a spelling element to be focused on, and provide sufficient examples to consolidate the teaching point. Topic words come from other curriculum areas, such as mathematics and social sciences. In addition, homophones and words that are easily confused with each other are explained and practised.

SLLURP

Each word list begins with a reminder for students to SLLURP. SLLURP summarises the strategies that will help spelling move from students' working memory to their long-term memory. These strategies are provided on page 2, for easy reference.

Unit at a glance

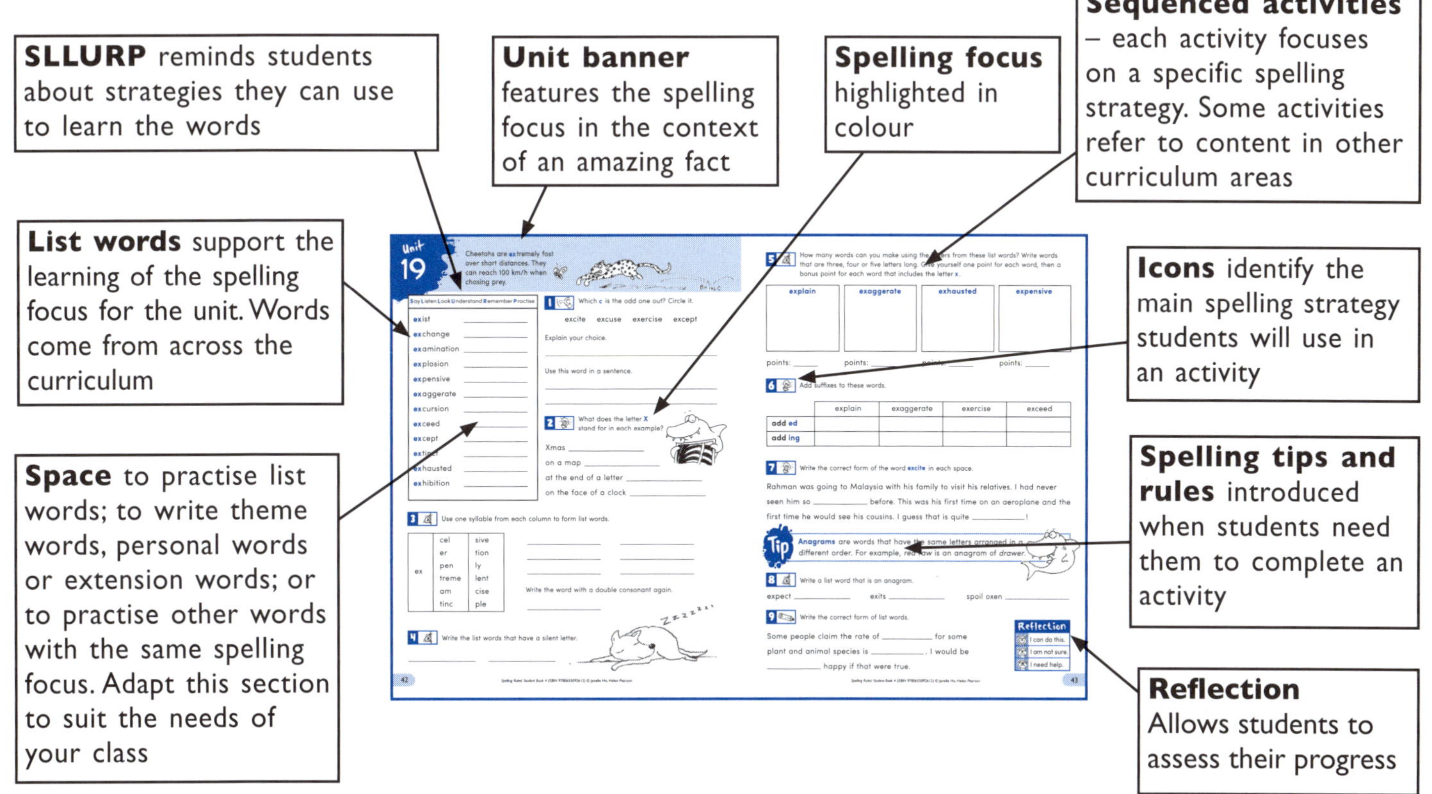

Spelling Rules! Teacher Resource Book 3–6

Full teacher support for *Student Book 4* is provided by *Spelling Rules! Teacher Resource Book 3–6*. Here you will find valuable background information about spelling development and spelling knowledge, along with practical resources, such as:

- teaching tips for every unit in *Student Book 4*
- extra word lists
- strategies for teaching spelling
- guidelines for assessment and diagnosis of errors
- activities to support struggling spellers
- worthwhile extension for more able spellers.

Unit 1

In China in 3000 BCE, children had powdered smallpox scabs stuck up their noses to make them immune to the horrible disease smallpox. It worked!

Say **L**isten **L**ook **U**nderstand **R**emember **P**ractise

- oppose ______
- endure ______
- revise ______
- complete ______
- arrange ______
- escape ______
- persuade ______
- realise ______
- collide ______
- assume ______
- include ______
- declare ______

1 Group list words using the final vowel sound.

a as in day

______
______
______

i as in by

______
______
______

e as in bead

______

o as in soap

______

u as in dew

______
______

list words left over

______
______

2 Write a list word that rhymes.

flows	strange	maid	replied	repair
______	______	______	______	______

3 Divide these list words into syllables. Underline the stressed syllable. For double consonants in the middle of a word, the syllable break comes between the double letters. *as/<u>sume</u>*

realise	suppose	declare	revise
arrange	conclude	collide	escape

Spelling Rules! Student Book 4 (ISBN 9780655092612) © Janelle Ho, Helen Pearson

Antonyms are words with opposite meanings. Make antonyms by adding missing letters.

in _ _ ude → e _ cl _ d _

ins _ _ t → del _ t _

inc _ ea _ e → d _ cr _ _ s _

s _ p _ _ ate → c _ mb _ n _

If a word ends in silent **e**, drop the **e** before adding the suffixes **ed** or **ing**.

Complete the table.

word	add ed	add ing
waste	wasted	wasting
oppose		
realise		
endure		
complete		
arrange		
collide		

6 Add **s**, **ed** or **ing** to the word in brackets.

No one ______________ the student dressed as a clown. (recognise)

'Stop ______________ me whenever you lose something!' Vicki yelled. (blame)

Each class is ______________ to perform an item at assembly. (require)

When a chess piece is captured, it is ______________ from the board. (remove)

Add vowels to make words that match the clues.

r _ sc _ _	save from danger	r _ m _ v _	take away
pr _ v _ d _	supply	_ ll _ str _ t _	draw
r _ t _ t _	turn		
p _ rf _ m _	pleasant fragrance		

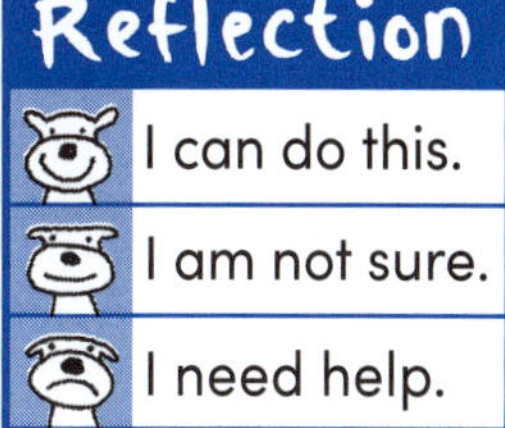

Spelling Rules! Student Book 4 (ISBN 9780655092612) © Janelle Ho, Helen Pearson

Unit 2

Nobody knows for certain how the pyramids in Egypt were built. It remains a mystery!

Say Listen Look Understand Remember Practise

copy	______
hurry	______
guilty	______
mystery	______
variety	______
deny	______
apply	______
simplify	______
qualify	______
display	______
prey	______
annoy	______

Rule If the word has a single vowel followed by a single consonant, double the consonant before adding **y**. *mud → muddy*

1 Make adjectives by adding **y**. Remember to follow the rule you have just learnt.

hair	shine	dirt
______	______	______
fur	risk	guilt
______	______	______
mess	spot	noise
______	______	______
itch	grub	droop
______	______	______

Rule If a word ends in **y**, change **y** to **i** before adding **es** or **ed**. Keep the **y** when adding **ing**.

2 Complete the table.

word	add es	add ed	add ing
hurry			
deny			
reply			
simplify			
qualify			

Spelling Rules! Student Book 4 (ISBN 9780655092612) © Janelle Ho, Helen Pearson

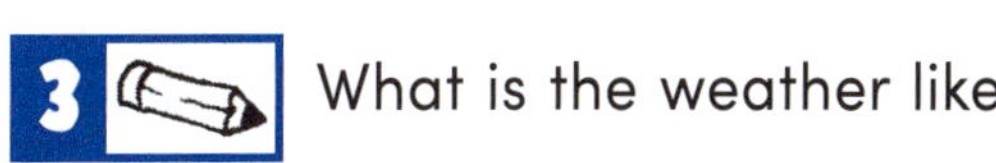

What is the weather like?

______________ ______________ ______________ ______________ ______________

Rewrite each sentence, replacing the underlined word with a list word.

Troy felt regretful that his ball had broken his neighbour's window.

____

Grandma's patchwork quilts have a range of colours and patterns.

____

What happened to Sally's keys is a puzzle.

____

Of all the animals on show, my favourite is the giraffe.

____

Don't bother Amy while she is coding her robot.

____

Rewrite each sentence in the plural.

There is only one variety of apple in the store.

____

Auntie made a copy of the recipe for Mum.

____

I have a fantasy about what I want to be when I grow up.

____

prey and **pray** are homophones. Write the correct homophone.

As the king of the jungle, the lion has many ______________.

You can't just ______________. You also have to work hard!

The plural form of **prey** does not change. Such words are known as

____

Spelling Rules! Student Book 4 (ISBN 9780655092612) © Janelle Ho, Helen Pearson

Unit 3

The left side of your body is control**l**ed by the right side of your brain.

Say Listen Look Understand Remember Practise

begin	________
forget	________
regret	________
occur	________
prefer	________
enter	________
offer	________
answer	________
visit	________
happen	________
target	________
label	________
detail	________

1  Each word has two syllables. Say each word and draw a line between the syllables. Underline the stressed syllable. *gal/<u>lop</u>*

begin regret occur

excel forget admit

Rule: When adding **ed** or **ing**, double the final consonant if:

1. the stress is on the final syllable and
2. the final syllable has one vowel.

occur → occurred, occurring

2  Complete the table.

add **ed**	add **ing**
travel ________	expel ________
permit ________	regret ________

Tip: The **schwa** is a short vowel sound that is very common in English. It sounds like 'uh'.

Rule: If the final syllable has two vowels, just add **ed** or **ing**.

appeal → appealed, appealing

3 Write the list words that have the schwa.

________ ________

________ ________

________ ________

4 Complete the table.

add **ed**	add **ing**
appear ________	complain ________
detail ________	reveal ________

Spelling Rules! Student Book 4 (ISBN 9780655092612) © Janelle Ho, Helen Pearson

Add a suffix to each list word. Use the rules to decide if the final consonant should be doubled. The stressed syllable is underlined.

word	add ed
prefer	
happen	
enter	
regret	
visit	
target	

word	add ing
begin	
forget	
offer	
occur	
label	
detail	

A word family consists of words that share the same base word.

act, actor, action, acting, acted, active, react

6 Complete each sentence using a word from the same word family as the word in brackets.

People sometimes get ______________ as they get older. (forget)

Mum is making a special dessert because we are having ______________. (visit)

Rani wanted to learn guitar so she joined a class for ______________. (begin)

Sean said he would meet me at the ______________ to the swimming pool. (enter)

You must wear ______________ goggles for this experiment. (safe)

7 Use list words to answer the questions.

Which word uses the same vowel sound twice? ______________

Which two words have the same meaning?

______________ and ______________

Reflection

- I can do this.
- I am not sure.
- I need help.

The fear of amphibians is known as batrachophobia.

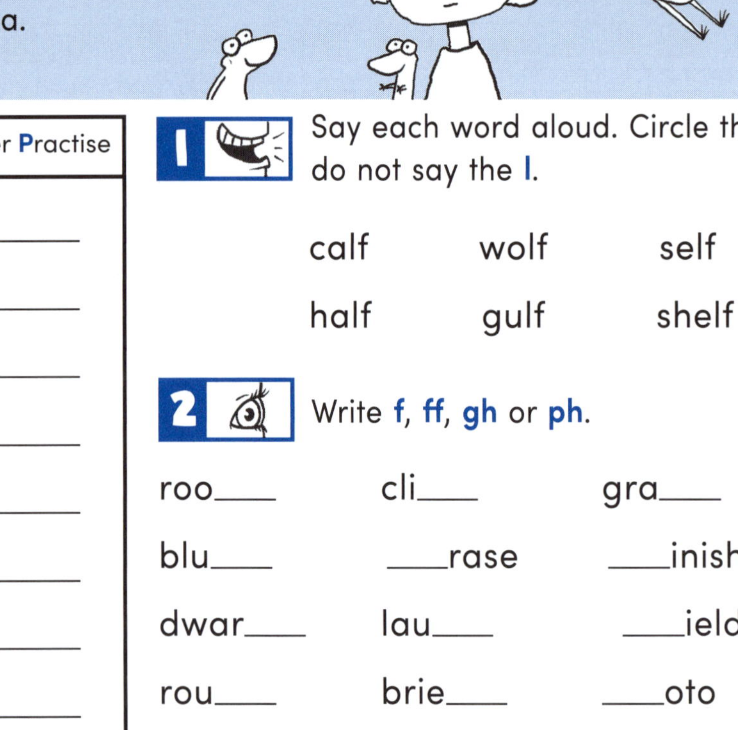

Say Listen Look Understand Remember Practise	
engulf	________
behalf	________
cough	________
trough	________
phase	________
phobia	________
phantom	________
metaphor	________
emphasise	________
biography	________
amphibian	________
sophisticated	________

1 Say each word aloud. Circle the word if you do not say the **l**.

calf wolf self

half gulf shelf

2 Write **f**, **ff**, **gh** or **ph**.

roo___ cli___ gra___

blu___ ___rase ___inish

dwar___ lau___ ___ield

rou___ brie___ ___oto

Which digraph cannot begin a word?

____

When a word ends in **f**, **lf** or **fe**, the **f** or **fe** usually changes to **v** before adding **es** to make the word plural.

leaf → leaves *elf → elves*

half → halves

When a word ends in **ff**, add **s** to make the word plural.

cliff → cliffs

Add **s** to make these words plural.

gulf → gulfs *proof → proofs*

chief → chiefs *belief → beliefs*

reef → reefs *roof → roofs*

3 Use the rules to write the plural word.

loaf ________

self ________

calf ________

hoof ________

sniff ________

wharf ________

4 Write the list words that are only nouns.

________ ________ ________ ________

________ ________ ________ ________

Spelling Rules! Student Book 4 (ISBN 9780655092612) © Janelle Ho, Helen Pearson

5 Use the clues to find **ph** words that complete the puzzle. Use a dictionary if you need help.

- a stage of development
- a group of words
- another word for ghost
- a wild bird you can eat
- a medical doctor
- a person who works in a pharmacy
- a person who studies philosophy

6 The word **phobia** is both a word and a word part. It can be combined with other word parts to describe different types of fear. Use a dictionary to write the meanings.

arachnophobia ______________________________

acrophobia ______________________________

nyctophobia ______________________________

ophidophobia ______________________________

7 Proofread this story. The text has five words that are incorrect. Circle the mistakes. Then write the correct spelling of the words in the boxes.

Mrs Berg's neffew tragically became an orfan when his parents died while swimming with dolfins. The dangers had been emfasised but their love of wildlife meant they took risks as fotografers. Ralph lives with the Bergs now.

8 Colour the correct word.

Our team scored a goal in each of the two | halfs | half's | halves | of the match.

I have so many books I need more | shelfs | shelf's | shelves |.

A | wolfs | wolf's | wolves | eyesight is better than a human's.

Cliff's | sniffs | sniff's | are loud and annoying.

Can we go fishing | of | off | the wharf on Saturday?

Reflection

- I can do this.
- I am not sure.
- I need help.

Levi Spear Parmly recommended using a waxen silk thread to floss. That was in 1819.

Say Listen Look Understand Remember Practise	
odd	____________
stiff	____________
err	____________
recall	____________
install	____________
swell	____________
thrill	____________
floss	____________
discuss	____________
possess	____________
witness	____________
embarrass	____________

Tip

A syllable that has double consonants at the end has a single vowel.

odd not *oodd*   *swell* not *sweell*

1 Correct the following words.

stieff	flooss	stil
____________	____________	____________
discuess	witnes	poesess
____________	____________	____________

2 Unscramble the letters to make a word that ends in a double consonant.

lrhitl	slepl	slnailt
____________	____________	____________
sarbs	fastf	darseds
____________	____________	____________

Tip

The suffixes **er** and **est** are added to words to compare two or more things.

kind kinder kindest

3 Add the word with the correct suffix.

It's odd to see Joe with short hair but it's ____________ to see him wearing a shirt and tie!

There are many dull books on the shelf. Unfortunately for me, I think I picked the ____________.

Tip

Some words that end in double consonants need to add **y** first.

mess messy messier messiest

4 Write the correct form of the adjective.

Jess says Ben is the ____________ player on the field. (boss)

Mr Cross is ____________ than Mr Bell about how we present our work. (fuss)

Spelling Rules! Student Book 4 (ISBN 9780655092612) © Janelle Ho, Helen Pearson

5  An anagram is a word or phrase in which the letters can be rearranged to form another word or phrase. Write a list word for each anagram.

nil salt ______ its news ______ caller ______ bears arms ______

6 Add the suffix.

	add **s** or **es**
chill	
add	
bluff	
witness	
discuss	

	add **ed**	add **ing**
swell		
install		
stuff		
stress		
embarrass		

7  Use the clues to write list words.

Which word has the antonym of short? ______

Which word has a donkey in it? ______

Which word has sickness in it? ______

Which word has the antonym of sickness? ______

8 Imagine you have witnessed a robbery. Write your eyewitness account.

______

______

______

______

______

9  *re + call = recall*

Write other words that use the prefix **re**.

______

______

 I can do this.

 I am not sure.

 I need help.

Spelling Rules! Student Book 4 (ISBN 9780655092612) © Janelle Ho, Helen Pearson

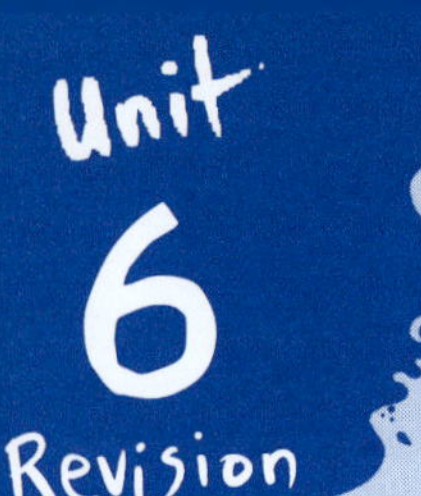

Laughter is great exercise. It increases your heart rate, lowers your blood pressure and gives your face and stomach muscles a good workout!

1 An **f** sound can be written as **f**, **ff**, **gh** or **ph**. Write the correct letter or letters to complete each word.

sni___	whar___	___rase	rou___	meta___or
behal___	lau___	o___ten	dwar___	autogra___

2 Sort the words into three groups.

target assume excite trophy disease surprise

verb only	verb or noun	noun only
___________	___________	___________
___________	___________	___________

3 Write the plural.

slide ___________

graph ___________

mystery ___________

shelf ___________

belief ___________

witness ___________

4 Write each verb so that it agrees with the new subject.

we annoy, she ___________

I prefer, it ___________

they forget, he ___________

you recognise, she ___________

I cough, he ___________

you qualify, she ___________

5 Write sentences. First use the word as a noun. Then use it as a verb.

laugh (noun) ______________________________

laugh (verb) ______________________________

visit (noun) ______________________________

visit (verb) ______________________________

6 Write an antonym.

exit ____________ admit ____________ exclude ____________

finish ____________ predator ____________ soften ____________

incomplete ____________ remember ____________ question ____________

7 Write the correct form of the word to complete each sentence.

Were you __________ when you won the prize? (surprise)

I had a most __________ holiday last summer. (excite)

We stopped when we saw Mr Tang __________ down the corridor. (hurry)

When our neighbour's cat meows, Rover __________ by barking. (reply)

The tennis final is __________ right now. I am __________ not bringing a hat to school because I am not __________ to sit with my class to watch it. (happen, regret, allow)

8 Write about something you did that you feel guilty about.

____

____

____

____

Unit 7

The average person has about 100 000 dreams in their lifetime.

Zzzz

Say Listen Look Understand Remember Practise	
least	______
eager	______
release	______
dread	______
ahead	______
heavy	______
health	______
meant	______
instead	______
pleasant	______
jealous	______
weather	______

1 Make words using the letters from each shape.

r l h thr spr tr

___ead ___ead ___ead

___ead ___ead ___ead

l lt f d th r

dea___ dea___ dea___

dea___ dea___ dea___

w sp st sn squ fr

___eak ___eak ___eak

___eak ___eak ___eak

2 Write the list words under the correct heading.

ea sound as in leaf

______

______

______

ea sound as in head

______ ______

______ ______

______ ______

______ ______

______

Spelling Rules! Student Book 4 (ISBN 9780655092612) © Janelle Ho, Helen Pearson

3 Make a new word. Circle the new word if the vowel sound has changed.

mean + t ____________ seat + w ____________ heal + th ____________ breath + e ____________ tread + h ____________

4 Write a list word with the same meaning.

talk ____________

keen ____________

unable to hear ____________

nice ____________

5 Write a list word with the opposite meaning.

illness ____________

most ____________

light ____________

behind ____________

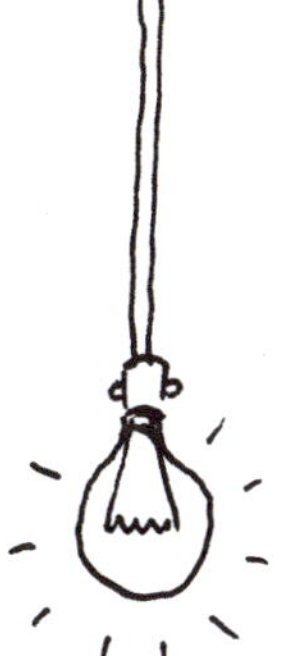

6 Write list words.

This New Year's Day we are going to a restaurant ____________ of having a picnic.

Regular visits to the dentist are important for our dental ____________.

7 *Weather* and *whether* are **homophones**. Write the correct word in each sentence.

Dean loves movies, ____________ they are dramas or comedies.

I hope the ____________ will be fine for our excursion.

Homographs are words with the same spelling but different meanings.

lead (sounds like bead) = go first, show someone the way

lead (sounds like head) = a heavy metal

In addition, the words *led* (the past tense of lead) and *lead* (a metal) are **homophones**.

8 Write a sentence for both meanings of *lead* and for *led*.

____

____

____

____

Unit 8

The average Australian eats around 6 kilograms of chocolate each year. That's a lot of Easter eggs!

Say **L**isten **L**ook **U**nderstand **R**emember **P**ractise

ginger	______
gently	______
general	______
average	______
generous	______
religion	______
intelligent	______
fragile	______
generation	______
advantage	______
emergency	______
gymnasium	______

1 Circle the letter **g** if it has a soft sound.

danger	regret	germ
eager	gigantic	logical

2 Fill in the missing vowels to make words with a soft **g** sound.

man _ g _

_ rr _ ng _

_ xyg _ n

eng _ n _ _ r

g _ psy

p _ ss _ ng _ r

_ r _ g _ n _ l

3 Group the list words as nouns, adjectives and adverbs. Use a dictionary if you need help. (Three words can be used as both nouns and adjectives.)

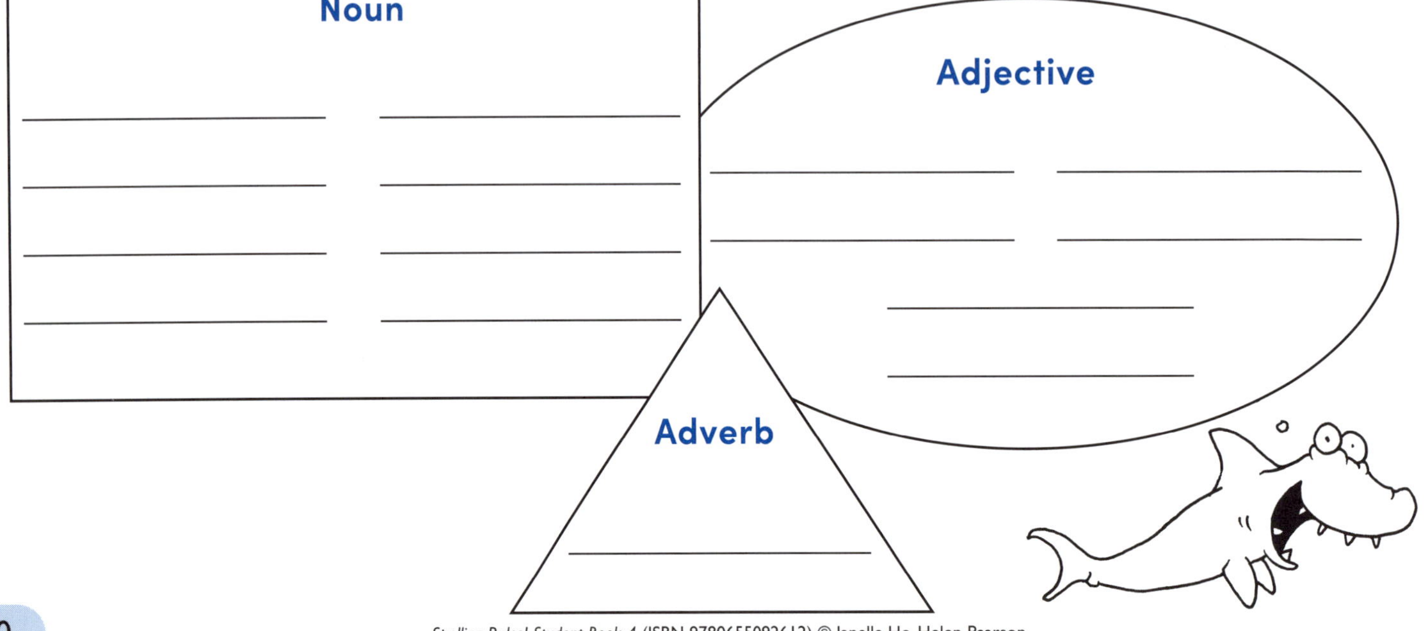

Spelling Rules! Student Book 4 (ISBN 9780655092612) © Janelle Ho, Helen Pearson

4 Add **ly** to make adverbs.

generous ________________ intelligent ________________

general ________________ gentle ________________

5 Make antonyms by adding **dis** or **un** as a prefix.

intelligent ______________ advantage ______________ original ______________

6 Choose the correct word to complete each sentence.

gymnast	gymnastics	gymnasium

A ______________ is a place where you do various sports and exercises.

______________ is a sport that includes vaulting and tumbling. You need to be strong to be a ______________.

7 Circle the word or words that do not make sense.
Write a list word that you could use instead.

Gerard is very general. He always shares things with his friends. ________________

I can hear sirens. Get out of the way! There must be an emerald. ________________

Angie has an adverb because she's played this game before. ________________

Our generator will be the first to live mainly in a digital world. ________________

8 Write an antonym that has a soft **g** sound.

foolish ______________ harsh ______________

special ______________ tough ______________

selfish ______________ copy ______________

specific ______________ small ______________

Reflection

- I can do this.
- I am not sure.
- I need help.

Unit 9

The Great Wall of China is so large it runs for more than 8000 kilometres!

Say **L**isten **L**ook **U**nderstand **R**emember **P**ractise

bandage	______
sponge	______
surge	______
stranger	______
siege	______
badger	______
pledge	______
reject	______
injection	______
adjust	______
conjunction	______
adjective	______

Rule

When **g** is followed by **e** or **i**, it usually makes a soft **g** sound.

page *magic* *giant*

But sometimes **g** before **e** or **i** makes a hard **g** sound.

gear *girl*

1 Group the words according to the sound **g** makes.

great angry ginger together
genius strange imagine agree

soft **g** ______ ______
______ ______

hard **g** ______ ______
______ ______

2 Write two words with the same vowel sound. Use a list word and a word of your own.

word	such	dirt	shame	wheel
list word				
my word				

Shark

Dark

3 Write list words.

Write the word that can be an adjective or a noun. ______

Write the words that are verbs only. ______ ______

4 Write the plural.

word	plural
bandage	
sponge	
siege	
stranger	
emergency	

5 Write the past tense.

word	past tense
surge	
pledge	
damage	
adjust	
budget	

6 Rearrange the letters to make a word. Each word has a soft **g** sound.

Angela pushed her ____________ (finger) off her face so she could see the actors on the ____________ (gates) more clearly. The hero was in great ____________ (garden).

Tip

A **conjunction** joins word, phrases or clauses. Here are some common conjunctions:

and nor but or so if because although

7 Write a conjunction to complete the sentence.

We are going to the local market to buy some meat ____________ fruit. We want to walk there ____________ it's raining, ____________ Dad insists we have to drive. Luckily, the rain becomes lighter. Dad agrees we can walk ____________ we each have a raincoat ____________ an umbrella.

8 Circle the mistake in each sentence. Write the correct word.

Lucy redjected Jim's apology because she was still angry. ________________

This year, every class will plege to raise $150. ________________

Our family gets our flu ingections every year. ________________

Use a soapy sponje to clean the stain. ________________

Only a jenius can solve the mystery! ________________

Reflection

- I can do this.
- I am not sure.
- I need help.

Unit 10

It is impossible to fold a **pie**ce of paper of almost any size in half more than seven times. Try it!

Say **L**isten **L**ook **U**nderstand **R**emember **P**ractise

ni**e**ce	______
bel**ie**f	______
ach**ie**ve	______
al**ie**n	______
rec**ei**pt	______
dec**ei**ve	______
prot**ei**n	______
w**ei**rd	______
r**ei**gn	______
s**ei**ze	______
b**ei**ge	______
f**ei**sty	______

1 Circle the words that don't have an **ee** sound (as in *see*).

weight	foreign	deceive
relieve	weird	reign
seize	fierce	achieve
sleigh	protein	alien

Tip

Have you heard that **i** comes before **e** except after **c**? Many words do not follow this rule.

2 Write the list words that don't follow the rule.

______ ______ ______

______ ______ ______

3 Fill in **ie** or **ei**.

bel___ve rec___ve ach___ve

w___rd h___ght c___ling

4 Write the correct word to complete each sentence.

beliefs
believes

Mr Johnson ______ that UFOs have visited Earth.

It is important to respect other people's ______.

relief
relieve

If you burn your skin, use cool water to ______ the pain.

When the lost girl found her parents, she cried with ______.

Spelling Rules! Student Book 4 (ISBN 9780655092612) © Janelle Ho, Helen Pearson

5 Write a sentence using each word.

receipt	______________________________
receive	______________________________

6 Draw a line to match each word with its meaning. If you need help, use a dictionary.

niece	vain or having a high opinion of yourself
foreign	mislead or trick
conceited	from another country
perceive	discover using one of your five senses
deceive	what a girl is to her aunt and uncle

7 One word in each sentence is missing the letter **e**. Find the word, fill in the missing **e** and write the word correctly.

My parents encourage me to size every opportunity to learn. ______________

Mr Yang has bought his nice Emma a necklace for Christmas. ______________

Janet was relived to discover her precious pet was safe. ______________

The foal will take a while to train because she is fisty. ______________

We must have clean hands at Grandpa's because the furniture is big. ______________

Rain, *rein* and *reign* are **homophones**.
rain = wet weather   *rein* = a strap to lead a horse   *reign* = royal rule

8 Colour the correct word.

Queen Elizabeth I of England never married during her long | rain | rein | reign |.

Use the | rains | reins | reigns | gently but firmly.

Heavy | rain | rein | reign | filled our new water tank.

Some turtles can **breathe** through their bottoms when underwater.

Say **L**isten **L**ook **U**nderstand **R**emember **P**ractise

lose	____________
loose	____________
breath	____________
breathe	____________
desert	____________
dessert	____________
practise	____________
practice	____________
wonder	____________
wander	____________
stationery	____________
stationary	____________

Tip

Homophones are words that sound the same but are spelt differently.

Some sets of words aren't homophones but do sound alike.

lose/loose

Some sets of words aren't homophones but look alike.

wander/wonder

1 Underline the pairs that are homophones. Check your dictionary if you are unsure.

his/he's	your/you're
there/their	angel/angle
were/we're	their/they're
weather/whether	whose/who's

Tip

Mnemonics are memory tricks. They help you remember something more easily. look, blood

Here are some mnemonics: *Lose an **o** from loose.*

*I'd like a **piece** of **pie**.* *I'd like a **s**econd **s**erve of de**ss**ert.*

2 Which list words are homophones?

____________ and ____________ ____________ and ____________

3 Make up your own mnemonics. You can write or draw.

breath/breathe	**practise/practice**	**wonder/wander**

Spelling Rules! Student Book 4 (ISBN 9780655092612) © Janelle Ho, Helen Pearson

4 Write the correct word.

wonder wander	Walkers like to ____________ in the bush reserve. I ____________ what our new teacher will be like.
where were	This is ____________ Abdul hurt himself. He and his friends ____________ skateboarding when he fell.
lose loose	Ellen lets her puppies run ____________ in the garden. She has to be careful not to ____________ them.
desert dessert	Grandma makes the best chocolate ____________ . The largest ____________ in the world is the Sahara.

5 Write a word from Activity 1 in each space.

'Y__________ not watching TV till you tidy y__________ room!' Mum told Linda. Linda had no choice. 'W__________ shirt is this?' she asked. 'W__________ been messing up my room?'

'Hurry up, sis!' Brian grumbled. 'W__________ going to miss the show. Wonderboy will meet h__________ enemy and I bet h__________ in real trouble without Zappa. T__________ such a great team!'

6 Write a sentence using both words.

course coarse	______________________________________ ______________________________________ ______________________________________
bored board	______________________________________ ______________________________________ ______________________________________

Reflection

- I can do this.
- I am not sure.
- I need help.

Unit 12 Revision

A cockroach can live up to ten days without a **head**, before dying of starvation.

Tip **Synonyms** are words that have the same meaning.

Tip **Antonyms** are words that are opposite in meaning.

1 Write a synonym.

keen ________________

train ________________

nice ________________

cheat ________________

flimsy ________________

fixed ________________

foreign ________________

2 Write an antonym.

light ________________

behind ________________

unique ________________

tight ________________

friend ________________

most ________________

accept ________________

3 Write the correct form of the verb to complete each sentence.

The players were so puffed that they were ____________ (breathe) heavily.

The stream ____________ (merge) with the river and finally flows into the sea.

'Do you know who ____________ (judge) the Spelling Bee?' Trish wondered.

Dad has ____________ (lose) his keys again!

At yesterday's assembly everyone ____________ (fidget) impatiently until the policeman ____________ (speak).

Spelling Rules! Student Book 4 (ISBN 9780655092612) © Janelle Ho, Helen Pearson

4 Write the words in the correct box.

eager	and	so	weird	but	jealous	loose	or

conjunction	**adjective**

5 Fill in **ge**, **dge** or **j**.

While building the extension to our house, Dad hurt his knee with a sle_____hammer. The doctor gave him an in_____ection to help with the pain. Now he has two banda_____s and won't bu_____ from his chair.

6 Remove a letter from each word to make a new word. Colour the circle if the two words have different vowel sounds.

○ close __________

○ least __________

○ niece __________

○ bridge __________

○ breathe __________

○ dealt __________

○ dessert __________

○ brain __________

7 Proofread this text. The text has five words that are incorrect. Circle the mistakes. Then write the correct spelling of the words in the boxes.

A biography about King Sami has just been relleased. He was the intelligent and fiesty prince who seized the throne from his father. His father was gilty of deseiving the people. In constrast, King Sami displayed a generus side during his reign. The people cannot recall a more popular king.

Unit 13

Cat's eyes glow at night because they reflect light. This makes it easier for them to see in the dark.

Say Listen Look Understand Remember Practise

narrow	______
sorrow	______
tomorrow	______
loan	______
poach	______
coward	______
foul	______
announce	______
voucher	______
boundary	______
council	______
knowledge	______

1 Sort the list words according to the sound that **ow** makes.

rhymes with snow	rhymes with cow
______	______
______	______
______	______
______	______
______	______
	______

Which list word is the odd one out?

______

2 Change one letter at a time to make the first word into the last word.

moved
______
______
towel

prowl
______
______
frown

3 Use a suffix from the box to make a new word. Use each suffix only once.

ship	s	ing	ly	er	ful

prowl ______
power ______
announce ______
town ______
coward ______
boundary ______

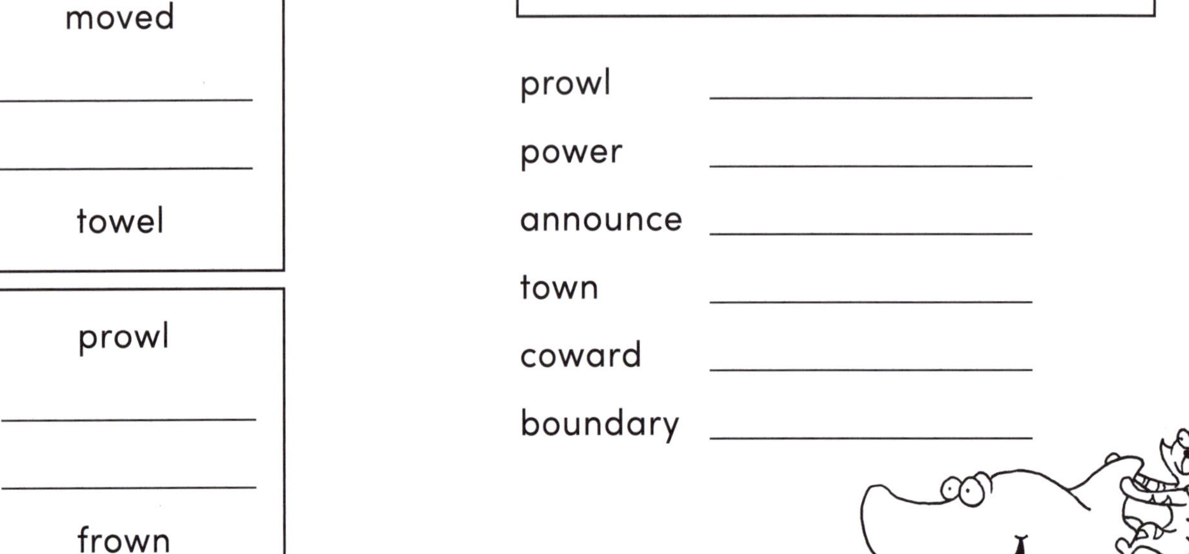

Spelling Rules! Student Book 4 (ISBN 9780655092612) © Janelle Ho, Helen Pearson

4 Use the clues to complete the puzzle.

1	O	W				
2		O	W			
3			O	W		
4				O	W	
5					O	W

1. If a thing belongs to you, you are the ________.

2. Use this to dry yourself.

3. You might do this if you are angry.

4. give permission or let something happen

5. neither broad nor wide

5 There is an error in each sentence. Circle the incorrect word and write it correctly.

We are having pooched chicken for dinner. ____________________

The councill is adding bicycle lanes to the main street. ____________________

The voucher can be used from tommorrow. ____________________

My favourite mystery books are out on lawn. ____________________

The boundery between the houses is marked by a fence. ____________________

6 *Foul* and *fowl* are **homophones**. Use each word in a sentence.

foul ____

fowl ____

7 Write a compound word with **ow** for each picture.

__________ + __________ = ______________

__________ + __________ = ______________

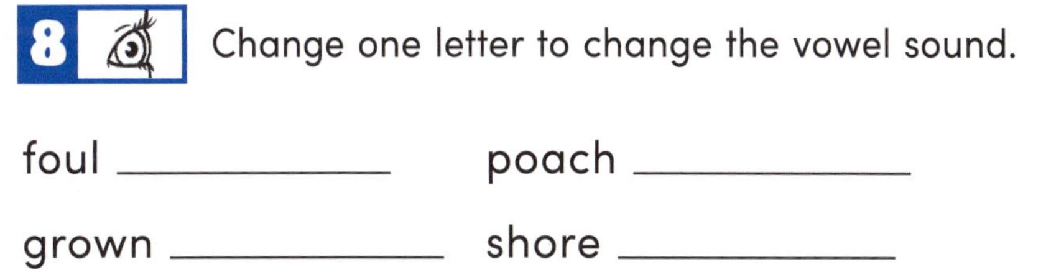

8 Change one letter to change the vowel sound.

foul ____________ poach ____________

grown ____________ shore ____________

Reflection

- I can do this.
- I am not sure.
- I need help.

Unit 14

The size of an **ear**thquake is measured using a seismograph.

Say **L**isten **L**ook **U**nderstand **R**emember **P**ractise

- verse ______
- superb ______
- alert ______
- convert ______
- deserve ______
- determined ______
- certain ______
- permanent ______
- earthquake ______
- research ______
- earnest ______
- rehearsal ______

1 Write a list word that rhymes but is spelt differently.

purse ______ perch ______ curve ______

2 Answer the questions.

Which two list words rhyme? ______ ______

Which list word has a prefix? ______

3 Write list words in each category.

Parts of a text	Character traits	Verbs
chapter	serious	
stanza		

4 *Certainly* and *perhaps* express how sure we are about an event happening. Arrange these words in order, from most likely to least likely.

definitely not   likely   maybe   certainly   probably not

______

5 Write a list word. You may need to add a suffix.

Max ______ his prize. His ______ project not only included detailed information but also had great pictures. It was ______. His ______ attitude to his work ______ helped him.

Spelling Rules! Student Book 4 (ISBN 9780655092612) © Janelle Ho, Helen Pearson

6 Look at the words in the box. What does each prefix mean?

reverse return
re means
____

research remarry
re means
____

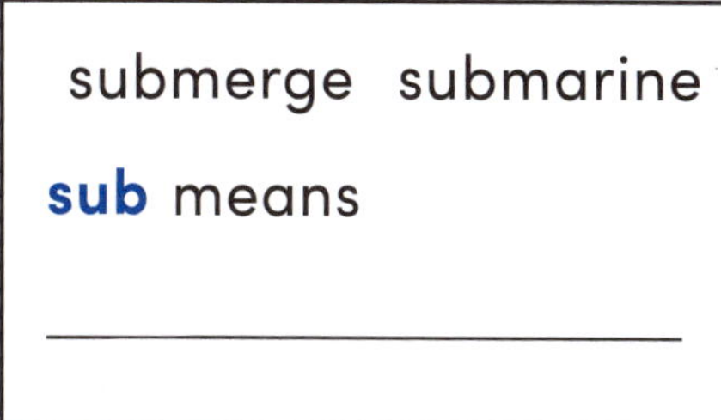
submerge submarine

sub means

____

7 Use the clues to complete the puzzle.

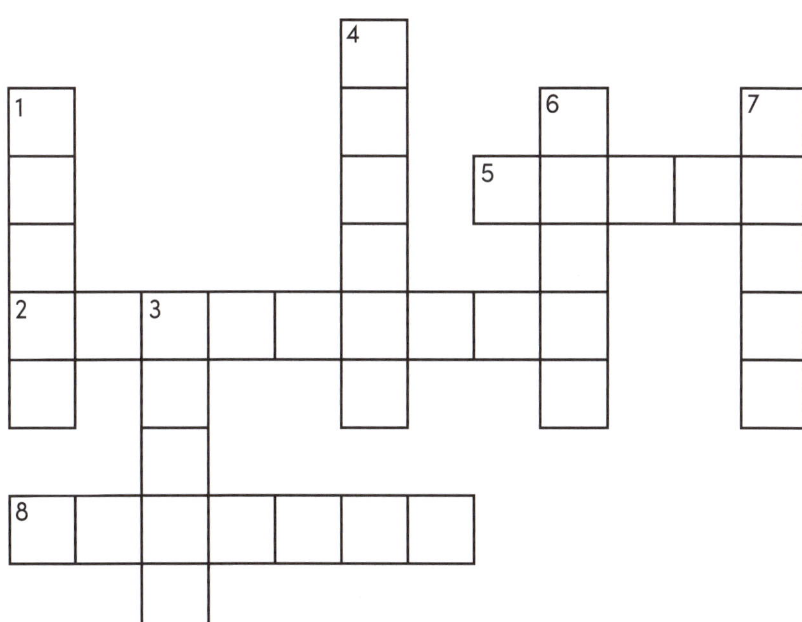

Down

1. attentive
3. past tense of hear
4. excellent
6. not late
7. first, second, ________________

Across

2. a practice for a performance
5. our planet
8. sincere

8 Is the underlined word a verb, noun or adjective?

The ringing <u>alerted</u> us to leave the building immediately. ________________

After a good night's sleep, he awoke refreshed and <u>alert</u>. ________________

I did not do much <u>research</u> for my project. ________________

The scientists want to <u>research</u> more animals before they write their report. ________________

Mali is the most <u>determined</u> girl I know. ________________

The teachers <u>determine</u> where the students will sit in the classroom. ________________

Reflection

I can do this.

I am not sure.

I need help.

Unit 15

The human intestine can stretch further than six metres!

Say Listen Look Understand Remember Practise	
worthy	
senior	
surprise	
further	
burden	
survive	
journal	
flavour	
labour	
courtesy	
honour	
harbour	

1 Say each word. Circle the words that have the **er** sound.

forth	four	word
sour	colour	bored
course	worry	porch

2  Answer the questions.

Which list word has a silent letter? ______________

Which list word has three syllables? ______________

One list word begins with the letter that another ends with. Write the two list words.

______________ ______________

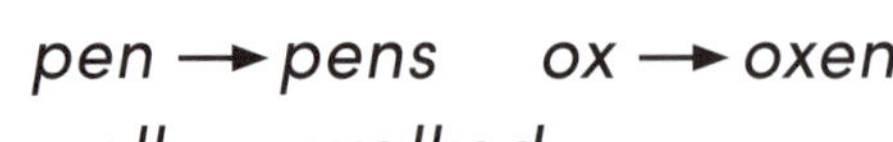

A **suffix** can:

- make a noun plural — *pen → pens* *ox → oxen*
- change the tense of a verb — *walk → walked*
- make a new part of speech — *fair → fairly, fairness, fairest*

3 Add the suffix.

worth + y → ______________

surprise + s → ______________

surprise + ing + ly → ______________

honour + ed → ______________

honour + able → ______________

survive + ed → ______________

survive + al → ______________

journal + ist → ______________

nourish + es → ______________

nourish + ment → ______________

Spelling Rules! Student Book 4 (ISBN 9780655092612) © Janelle Ho, Helen Pearson

4 There is an error in each sentence. Circle the incorrect word and then write it correctly.

Eggs are a nurrishing breakfast. ____________

They are healthy and full of flaver. ____________

Mum will be late to my rehersal. ____________

She has ferther to travel. ____________

She works at a hospital as a senior nerse. ____________

5 Write a list word to complete these book titles and authors.

My Home Recipes by Full O. ____________

Food in the ____________ by Fisher Mann

How to be prepared for anything by No ____________

Do the right thing! by ____________ Able

Hard Yakka! by ____________ Day

Tip

Etymology is the study of the origin of words.
For example, *cricket* comes from an old French word *criquet*, meaning *stick*.

6 *Courtesy, courteous* and *courtship* all have the base word *court*. This *court* is the court of a king.
Use your dictionary to find the meaning of each word, then use it in your own sentence.

courtesy ____________

courteous ____________

courtship ____________

7 Answer the questions in full sentences.

What is your surname?

____

Which suburb do you live in?

____

Reflection

I can do this.

I am not sure.

I need help.

Unit 16

Even though Mercury is the closest planet to the sun, its temperat**ure** can fall to –183°C. That is much colder than it ever gets here on Earth!

Say **L**isten **L**ook **U**nderstand **R**emember **P**ractise

nat**ure**	____________
fut**ure**	____________
capt**ure**	____________
fail**ure**	____________
creat**ure**	____________
feat**ure**	____________
meas**ure**	____________
pleas**ure**	____________
leis**ure**	____________
advent**ure**	____________
furnit**ure**	____________
temperat**ure**	____________

1 Write the words. Draw an arrow pointing to the word that has a different middle consonant sound.

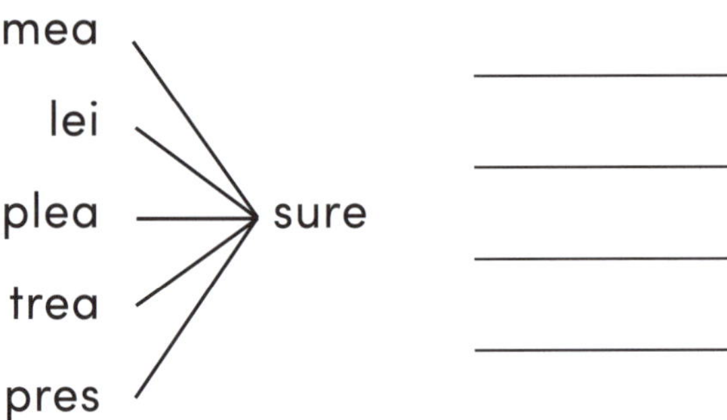

mea
lei
plea → sure
trea
pres

____
____
____
____
____

2 Write the words.

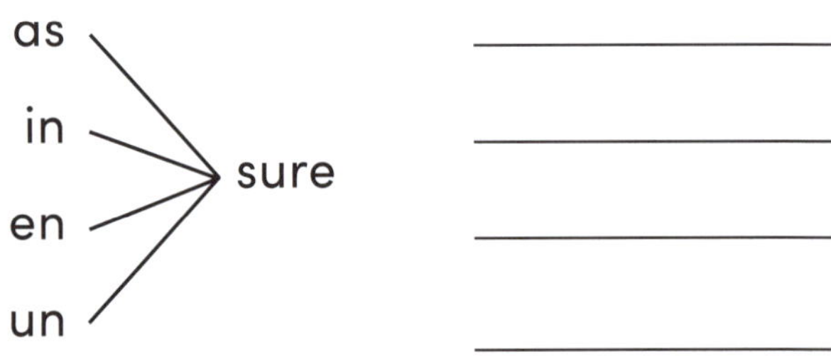

as
in → sure
en
un

____
____
____
____

3 Add the suffix. Use the new word in a sentence. Use a dictionary if you need help.

leisure + ly → ____________

____

measure + ing → ____________

____

measure + ment → ____________

____

nature + al → ____________

____

Spelling Rules! Student Book 4 (ISBN 9780655092612) © Janelle Ho, Helen Pearson

4 Write the base words.

failure	pleasure	signature	naturally	impure
______	______	______	______	______

 **5** Use each clue to write a word ending in **ure**. Only some are list words.

1. to heal, make well

2. sky blue colour

3. It may happen in the ________ .

4. time to do what you like

5. precious object

6. tables, chairs, beds

6 Write list words.

Week-long hikes in ____________ reserves give my aunt and uncle a great deal of ____________ .

The last time I had a fever my ____________ rose to 39 °C.

My family played Monopoly by candlelight during the power______________ .

I wish I could have an ____________ holiday on safari in Africa.

 **7** Answer the questions.

Temperature is measured with a thermometer.

thermo- is a word part from the Greek word *thermos*, which means ____________ .

-meter is a word part from the Greek word *metron*, which means ____________ .

Underwear that keeps you warm is known as ____________ underwear.

The length of the outside of a shape is its ____________ .

Unit 17

The colours of the rainbow are **r**ed, **o**range, **y**ellow, **g**reen, **b**lue, **i**ndigo and **v**iolet. When you want to remember it, think of Roy G Biv!

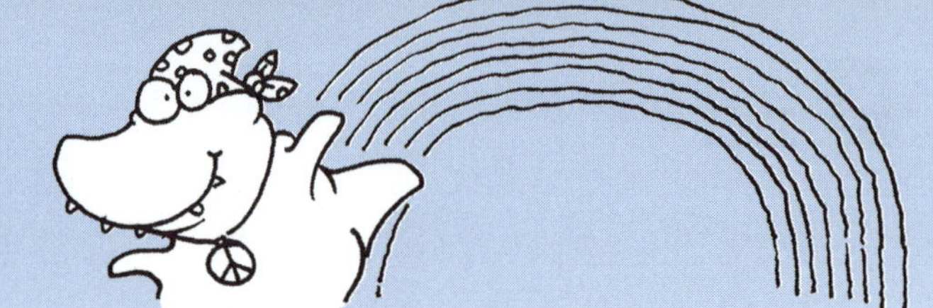

Say **L**isten **L**ook **U**nderstand **R**emember **P**ractise

ruby	______
scarlet	______
lilac	______
violet	______
emerald	______
indigo	______
crimson	______
azure	______
khaki	______
ochre	______
turquoise	______
sapphire	______

1 The names of colours often come from nature. Group the colour words from the list. Write the common name for each colour in the brackets. Use a dictionary to help you.

From flowers: ______ (______)
______ (______)

From gems: ______ (______)
______ (______)
______ (______)
______ (______)

From earth: ______ (______)

2 Think of other ways to group the colours. Use the space below to arrange your groups. Write a title for each group.

3 Use a dictionary to find words with *aqua*.

What does *aquamarine* mean? ______

What does *aqua* mean? ______

Write more words with *aqua*. ______

Spelling Rules! Student Book 4 (ISBN 9780655092612) © Janelle Ho, Helen Pearson

4 Write a list word to describe each noun.

_______________ sky   _______________ lips   _______________ sea

_______________ land   _______________ eyes   _______________ blood

5 Use the clues to find a list word.

This colour has all the vowels except **a**. _______________

The first syllable of this colour is a mark left after you've hurt yourself. _______________

The word for this colour is Urdu in origin. _______________

Add one letter to *call* and rearrange the letters to make this colour. _______________

This colour is important to First Nations Australians. _______________

6 What do these expressions mean?

to feel blue _______________   to see red _______________

to be a black sheep _______________

a white elephant _______________

to have a green thumb _______________

a golden opportunity _______________

Tip

Similes compare one thing to another. They say that one thing is *like* another.   *as red as a tomato*   *as white as snow*

7 Make up your own similes.

as blue as _______________   as _______________ as _______________

as green as _______________   as _______________ as _______________

as yellow as _______________   as _______________ as _______________

as black as _______________   as _______________ as _______________

Reflection

I can do this.

I am not sure.

I need help.

Unit 18 Revision

A tree measur**ed** in 1780 had a circumference of 57.9 metres. It held the world record for a long time.

1 Write the plural.

coward ________________

journey ________________

machine ________________

ruby ________________

church ________________

rehearsal ________________

patient ________________

furniture ________________

knowledge ________________

boundary ________________

2 Complete the tables.

verb	add **ed**	add **ing**
poach		
allow		
alert		

verb	add **ed**	add **ing**
burden		
honour		
capture		

3 Add **er**, **ir**, **or**, **ur** or **ear** to complete each word.

Susu h____d yet another balloon b____st. She had already blown up th____ty but the wind knew no m____cy! She was conc____ned that by the time the last p____son arrived at her b____thday party, the only s____viv____s would be the balloons still in the packet.

4 Each sentence has one wrong word. Circle the word. Change one or more letters in the word to make a new word that fits the sentence.

I hope that in the feature, greenhouse gases won't be a problem. ________________

'Can you azure me that the leak can be fixed?' Dad asked the plumber. ________________

'I am curtain of that,' the plumber replied. ________________

I had to interview my grandparents as part of my rehearse for a project. ________________

The tigers look majestic as they frown in their enclosure. ________________

Spelling Rules! Student Book 4 (ISBN 9780655092612) © Janelle Ho, Helen Pearson

5 Write some unusual colour words for each of the common colours.

blue	green	red	yellow	brown

6 Write an antonym.

broad ______________

release ______________

hero ______________

accept ______________

unaware ______________

success ______________

7 Make adverbs by adding the suffix **ly**.

narrow ______________

worthy ______________

loose ______________

certain ______________

usual ______________

gentle ______________

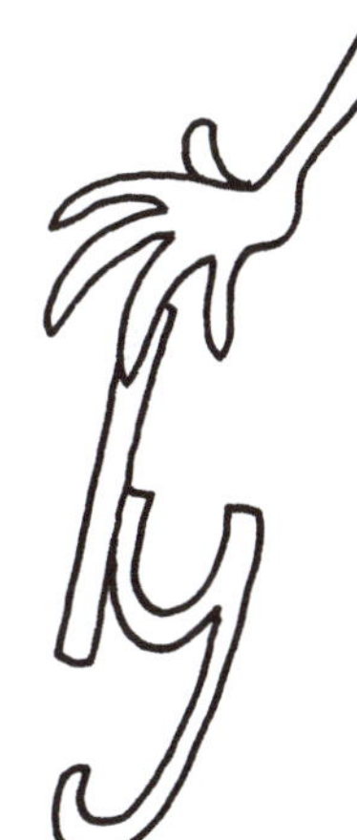

8 Use the clues to complete the puzzle. Write the hidden word.

1. good manners
2. a soft cloth for drying
3. a precious green stone
4. not ordinary
5. extremely old
6. the day after today
7. let or permit
8. all things not made by people
9. a long trip
10. an angry facial expression
11. maybe

Hidden word: ______________________________

Unit 19

Cheetahs are **ex**tremely fast over short distances. They can reach 100 km/h when chasing prey.

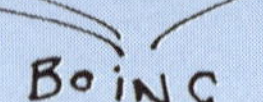

Say **L**isten **L**ook **U**nderstand **R**emember **P**ractise

exist	______
exchange	______
examination	______
explosion	______
expensive	______
exaggerate	______
excursion	______
exceed	______
except	______
extinct	______
exhausted	______
exhibition	______

1 Which **c** is the odd one out? Circle it.

excite excuse exercise except

Explain your choice.

____

Use this word in a sentence.

____

____

2 What does the letter **X** stand for in each example?

Xmas ______________

on a map ______________

at the end of a letter ______________

on the face of a clock ______________

3 Use one syllable from each column to form list words.

ex	cel	sive
	er	tion
	pen	ly
	treme	lent
	am	cise
	tinc	ple

______________ ______________

______________ ______________

______________ ______________

Write the word with a double consonant again.

____

4 Write the list words that have a silent letter.

______________ ______________

Spelling Rules! Student Book 4 (ISBN 9780655092612) © Janelle Ho, Helen Pearson

5 How many words can you make using the letters from these list words? Write words that are three, four or five letters long. Give yourself one point for each word, then a bonus point for each word that includes the letter **x**.

explain	exaggerate	exhausted	expensive

points: ______ points: ______ points: ______ points: ______

6 Add suffixes to these words.

	explain	exaggerate	exercise	exceed
add ed				
add ing				

7 Write the correct form of the word **excite** in each space.

Rahman was going to Malaysia with his family to visit his relatives. I had never seen him so ____________ before. This was his first time on an aeroplane and the first time he would see his cousins. I guess that is quite ____________!

Tip **Anagrams** are words that have the same letters arranged in a different order. For example, *red raw* is an anagram of *drawer*.

8 Write a list word that is an anagram.

expect ____________ exits ____________ spoil oxen ____________

9 Write the correct form of list words.

Some people claim the rate of ____________ for some plant and animal species is ____________. I would be ____________ happy if that were true.

Reflection

- I can do this.
- I am not sure.
- I need help.

Unit 20

Diseases of the heart and blood vessels are the leading cause of death in the world.

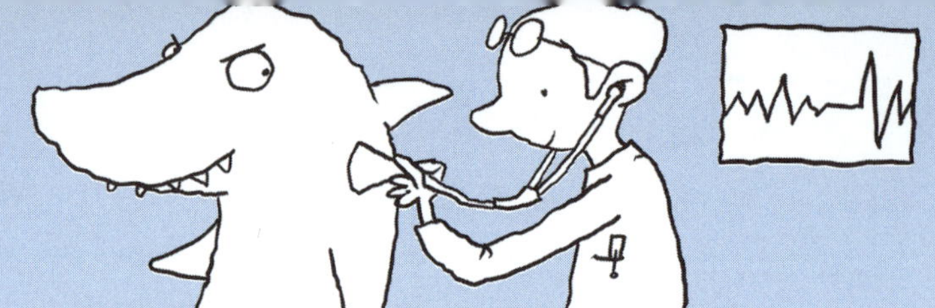

Say Listen Look Understand Remember Practise	
unfamiliar	________
undeveloped	________
unbroken	________
unquestioning	________
inactive	________
incomplete	________
informal	________
invisible	________
disease	________
disqualify	________
discontented	________
discontinue	________

Tip A prefix is placed in front of a word and changes its meaning. **un-**, **in-** and **dis-** are all prefixes.

1 Write the list words as prefix + base word. One has been done for you.

unfamiliar → un + familiar

undeveloped → ____ + ________

unbroken → ____ + ________

unquestioning → ____ + ________

inactive → ____ + ________

incomplete → ____ + ________

informal → ____ + ________

invisible → ____ + ________

disease → ____ + ________

disqualify → ____ + ________

discontented → ____ + ________

discontinue → ____ + ________

Tip A suffix is added to the end of a word. **-s**, **-ed**, **-ing**, **-er**, **-ion** and **-ness** are suffixes.

2 Break the words up into base word + suffix. Write another word by changing or adding a suffix.

developed ________ + ____ ________

questioning ________ + ____ ________

contented ________ + ____ ________

active ________ + ____ ________

formal ________ + ____ ________

Spelling Rules! Student Book 4 (ISBN 9780655092612) © Janelle Ho, Helen Pearson

The word *visible* means *capable of being seen*. It comes from the Latin word *videre*, which means *to see*.

3 Use a word from the box to complete the sentences.

vision	visual	visible

Tina has 20/20 ______________, which means she can see perfectly.

Jupiter is sometimes ______________ on a clear night in the country.

I love walks that provide ______________ guides about which animals and plants to look out for.

4 These sentences are silly. Rewrite them using a list word. You may need to add a suffix.

The council wants to build a school in the green busy field.

____

Mum is annoyed because I've finished my homework.

____

Joey started running before the whistle, so he was awarded first prize.

____

Ellen couldn't sing the song without looking at the words because she knew it by heart.

____

Tom's party is a fancy dress party, so it will be serious.

____

5 Write **dis**, **in** or **un**.

_____easy

_____please

_____organised

_____likely

_____appoint

_____accurate

_____comfortable

_____dependent

Unit 21

Before the compass was invented, explorers worked out the direct**ion**s using the sun during the day and the stars at night.

Say **L**isten **L**ook **U**nderstand **R**emember **P**ractise

reject**ion**	________
suggest**ion**	________
locat**ion**	________
separat**ion**	________
confus**ion**	________
decis**ion**	________
conclus**ion**	________
great**ness**	________
selfish**ness**	________
stubborn**ness**	________
cleanli**ness**	________
forgetful**ness**	________

Some verbs can be changed into nouns by adding **ion**.

act → action

If the verb ends in silent **e**, drop the **e** before adding **ion**.

create → creation

1  Complete the table.

verb	noun
complete	
	rejection
	confusion
perfect	
	separation
	prevention
locate	
relate	

Rule

If the verb ends in **de**, change **de** to **s** before adding **ion**.

divide → division

2  Write the noun to complete each sentence.

In most sports, the referee's ________ is final. (decide)

Olga wrote an exciting ________ to her story. (conclude)

The ________ of Sammi probably helped us win the Spelling Bee. (include)

There was a loud ________, but luckily no one was hurt. (explode)

Spelling Rules! Student Book 4 (ISBN 9780655092612) © Janelle Ho, Helen Pearson

Each word has one or two suffixes. Circle each suffix.

careless ness

greatness thoughtlessness stubbornness forgetfulness

Add either **ion** or **ness** to make a noun. Use a dictionary if you need help.

awkward ______________ dizzy ______________ desperate ______________

discuss ______________ cheerful ______________ extend ______________

The word *conclude* means *to come to an end*. It comes from the Latin word *claudere*, which means *to close*.

Add the correct prefix. Use the definitions to help you.

_____clude: contain or add to _____clude: keep out or leave out

These words are opposite in meaning. They are ______________

Write a sentence using one of the words.

____

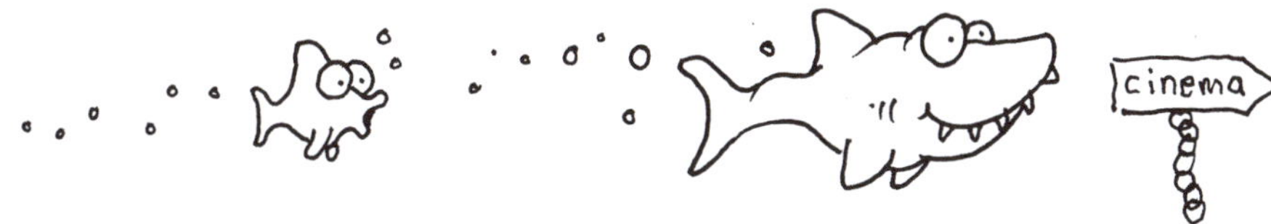

These sentences are too long. Rewrite them using a list word. The underlined words in the first two sentences are hints.

Can you tell me <u>in what street or building I would find</u> the cinema?

____

Writing our project was hard because Eng <u>refused to change his mind about some things</u>.

____

I often ask my family for their thoughts and ideas for my writing.

____

All cafés receive a rating based on how clean they are.

____

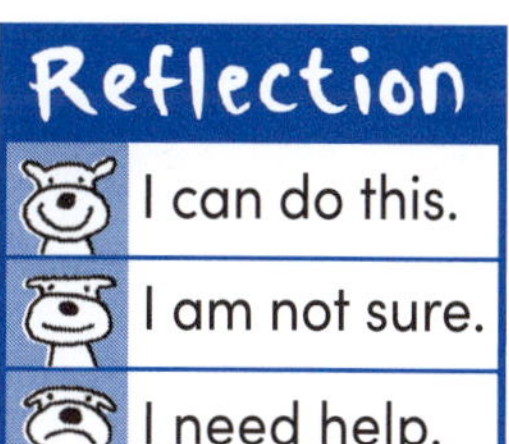

Unit 22

Ants have a lot of strength for their size. Some ants can drag objects that are 25 times their own weight.

Say **L**isten **L**ook **U**nderstand **R**emember **P**ractise

fourth	______
fifth	______
eighth	______
ninth	______
twelfth	______
growth	______
warmth	______
length	______
strength	______
width	______
depth	______
breadth	______

Rule Most numbers add **th** to make the adjective form.

1 Write an adjective for each numeral.

1 ______ 2 ______

3 ______ 4 ______

5 ______ 6 ______

7 ______ 8 ______

9 ______ 10 ______

11 ______ 12 ______

2 Write two number adjectives that drop letters before adding **th**. Write the dropped letter or letters in the box.

______ ☐ ______ ☐

Rule Some words add **th** to make the noun form.

grow → *growth*

The vowel or vowels sometimes change too.

deep → *depth*

3 Add **th** to make the noun form.

warm ______ long ______ wide ______

true ______ strong ______ broad ______

young ______

Which nouns keep the vowels but sound different?

______

Spelling Rules! Student Book 4 (ISBN 9780655092612) © Janelle Ho, Helen Pearson

Fill in the missing adjectives.

If Monday is the first day of the week, Thursday is the ____________ day.

August is the ____________ month of the year.

The letter **i** is the ____________ letter of the alphabet.

On your ____________ birthday, you celebrate a decade of life.

Venus is the ____________ planet from the Sun.

A centenary celebration marks the ____________ year of an event.

5 Write list words.

Use a ruler to measure the ____________ of wrapping paper you need.

Steel is a strong metal. Its ____________ makes it an ideal building material.

Rule

Numbers that end in **ty** change **y** to **i** and add **eth**.

twenty → *twentieth* *sixty* → *sixtieth*

6 Write the adjective for each numeral.

7 ____________ 10 ____________ 14 ____________

30 ____________ 40 ____________ 50 ____________

21 ____________ 82 ____________ 75 ____________

Fourth and *forth* are **homophones**. Colour the correct word.

This is the | fourth | forth | time I've seen this movie.

The lion was pacing back and | fourth | forth | in his cage.

Spelling Rules! Student Book 4 (ISBN 9780655092612) © Janelle Ho, Helen Pearson

Unit 23

If a cat has hair standing up on its body and tail and its back is arched, watch out – it's **agg**ress**ive**!

Say Listen Look Understand Remember Practise

a**cc**ept	________
a**pp**eal	________
stu**bb**orn	________
vi**ll**ain	________
po**ll**ute	________
a**pp**roach	________
o**pp**ortunity	________
a**tt**itude	________
nece**ss**ary	________
reco**mm**end	________
o**cc**asion	________
a**gg**re**ss**ive	________

1

Add a suffix from the box to each base word. Use each suffix at least once.

ness	ion	tion	ly	ment	able

stubborn	________
pollute	________
embarrass	________
approach	________
aggressive	________
disappoint	________
accuse	________
necessary	________
recommend	________

Rule

g and **c** make their soft sound when they are followed by **e** or **i**.

2

Circle the word in each pair that includes a soft consonant sound.

suggest	aggressive	accent	recount
accuse	accept	occasion	accident

3

These sentences have too many double letters. Rewrite each sentence correctly.

I've allways bellieved that ice cream is neccessarry for good health.

____

There's a speccial occassion this Saturday. It's Grandpa's seventty-fifth birthday!

____

Spelling Rules! Student Book 4 (ISBN 9780655092612) © Janelle Ho, Helen Pearson

4 Add a prefix to make an antonym.

_____ + appear → ______________ _____ + necessary → ______________

5 Add a suffix to make the correct form of the verb.

The lights turned red as I ______________. (approach)

The crowd didn't like it when the batsman ______________ the umpire's call for such a long time. (appeal)

Tomorrow the principal is ______________ who the school captain will be. (announce) I think it will be Cassie because she ______________ all the right qualities. (possess)

You are ______________ me! (embarrass)

Tip

Except and **accept** are often confused.

except = not including *accept* = take or receive

Affect and **effect** are also often confused.

affect = to cause a change in something *effect* = a result

6 Write the correct words to complete each sentence.

accept
except

Everyone in the family ______________ her grandmother was in the hall to see Ellen ______________ her award.

affect
effect

The things we do ______________ the environment. Pollution has a long-lasting ______________.

7 Use the clues to write a list word.

Which word has a harbour in it? ______________

Which word has a survey in it? ______________

Which word has a synonym for repair? ______________

Which word has a type of house in it? ______________

Reflection

I can do this.

I am not sure.

I need help.

Adults have around five **million** hairs all over their bodies – that's about the same number as a gorilla!

1 Write the missing words.

4 m

12 m

The ____________ of the rectangular garden is 12 metres.

Its ____________ is 4 metres.

The breadth of something is the same as its ____________.

2 Write a number word or number adjective to complete each sentence.

There are ____________ letters in the English alphabet, of which ____________ are consonants. The ____________ letter is a and the ____________ one is e.

There are three ____________ and ____________ days in a leap year. A year is divided into ____________ months. August, the ____________ month, has ____________ days.

3 Write double consonants to complete each word.

a___roach	a___use	po___e___	su___est	emba___a___
a___ounce	a___ear	sa___hire	pre___ure	tomo___ow

4 Write the base word. Then write a sentence using either word.

separation ____________ ______________________________

cleanliness ____________ ______________________________

unquestioning ____________ ______________________________

discontented ____________ ______________________________

5 Use each word in a sentence.

accept ______________________________

except ______________________________

Spelling Rules! Student Book 4 (ISBN 9780655092612) © Janelle Ho, Helen Pearson

6 Use the clues to complete the puzzle.

1. A good diet prevents _____ .
2. His nose is his strongest _____ .
3. A heater provides _____ when it's cold.
4. You win silver if you come _____ .
5. After ninety-nine comes one _____ .
6. Queen Elizabeth II had the longest _____ .
7. Dinosaurs are _____ .
8. There are _____ days in April.

Ants have great ____________________ for their size.

Replace the underlined word or words with a more interesting list word you have learnt. Rewrite the sentence using the correct form of the new word.

Jenny really wants to go to the circus.

____

Grandpa has a watch that winds without him having to do it.

____

If you go near their babies, animals will act as if they want to fight.

____

The clothes didn't fit, so Mum had to bring them back to the shop and get another pair that fit.

____

If I had a super power, I would like to not be able to be seen by others.

____

In that movie, the main evil character was my favourite character.

____

Can you not make everything seem worse or better than it really is?

____

Unit 25

Several centuries ago, **barbers** also did the work of surgeons and dentists.

Say **L**isten **L**ook **U**nderstand **R**emember **P**ractise

auth**or**	______
groc**er**	______
carpent**er**	______
lawy**er**	______
assist**ant**	______
account**ant**	______
electric**ian**	______
politic**ian**	______
journal**ist**	______
pharmac**ist**	______
chef	______
pilot	______

1 Use the picture as a clue for each occupation.

Tip The names of occupations are often base words with a suffix added.

wait + er → waiter *serve + ant → servant*

music + ian → musician *art + ist → artist*

2 Write the base word.

lawyer ______

engineer ______

journalist ______

physiotherapist ______

scientist ______

builder ______

assistant ______

politician ______

conductor ______

farmer ______

pharmacist ______

actor ______

Spelling Rules! Student Book 4 (ISBN 9780655092612) © Janelle Ho, Helen Pearson

Each word has the wrong ending. Write each word correctly.

docter ________________	photographist ________________
magicist ________________	dentant ________________
instructant ________________	drivor ________________
accountist ________________	electricant ________________

Apostrophes can be used to show who something belongs to. In other words, apostrophes can show **possession**.

*the pilot'**s** suitcase* (one pilot + one suitcase)

*the pilot'**s** duties* (one pilot + more than one duty)

When the owner is plural, the apostrophe comes **after** the plural. When the plural ends in **s**, do not add a second **s** after the apostrophe.

*the pilots**'** uniforms* (more than one pilot + more than one uniform)

*the children'**s** toys* (more than one child + more than one toy)

Add the missing apostrophes. Circle the words where the apostrophe does not show possession.

I needed a present for my friends birthday, so I thought Id look in Mr and Mrs Tangs new bookshop. Its called The Reading Room. It was crowded but I could tell from the customers smiles that they were enjoying themselves. The displays bright colours made the books look exciting. I saw one boys mother buy him four books! Im sure the shop will be a success.

Some English words come from other languages.

Write the meanings. Use a dictionary if you need help.

chef ____

chauffeur ____

What language are these words originally from? ________________

Unit 26

A skunk will spray you with very smelly liquid if you make it nerv**ous**!

Say **L**isten **L**ook **U**nderstand **R**emember **P**ractise

seri**ous** ______
preci**ous** ______
delici**ous** ______
fam**ous** ______
nerv**ous** ______
danger**ous** ______
courage**ous** ______
furi**ous** ______
cauti**ous** ______
envi**ous** ______
spaci**ous** ______
vari**ous** ______

1 Write the list word that comes from the same word family.

vary ______
courage ______
space ______
fame ______
danger ______
envy ______
nerve ______
fury ______
caution ______
deliciously ______
seriousness ______

2 Colour the correct word.

Words that end in **ous** are | adjectives | nouns | adverbs |.

Rule

When the base word ends in silent **e**, drop the **e** before adding **ous**.

fame → famous

If the base word ends in **ce**, change the **e** to **i** before adding **ous**.

space → spacious

3 Make an adjective by adding the suffix **ous**.

adventure → ______
grace → ______
ridicule → ______
vice → ______

Spelling Rules! Student Book 4 (ISBN 9780655092612) © Janelle Ho, Helen Pearson

If the base word ends in **ge**, keep the **e** when adding **ous** to keep the **g** sound soft. *courage → courageous*

4 Make an adjective by adding the suffix **ous**.

outrage → ____________ advantage → ____________

Rule

If the base word ends in **y**, change **y** to **i** before adding **ous**.
envy → envious *vary → various*

5 Make an adjective by adding the suffix **ous**.

fury → ____________ mystery → ____________

glory → ____________ luxury → ____________

6 Write list words.

Recently I watched a program about a ____________ athlete. She had suffered a ____________ accident, which caused her to lose both legs. However, she was very ____________. She overcame her disability to represent her country in the Paralympic Games. In an interview, she said that she still felt ____________ and had butterflies in her stomach before each race. The medals she has won at the Games and in other competitions are among her most ____________ possessions.

7 Write list words.

A person who is well-known is ____________.

A person who is extremely angry is ____________.

A person who doesn't take risks is ____________.

A person who wants what someone else has is ____________.

Food that people want to eat is ____________.

An activity that is unsafe is ____________.

Reflection

- I can do this.
- I am not sure.
- I need help.

Unit 27

The retire**ment** age in Australia is now 67.

Say Listen Look Understand Remember Practise	
invest**ment**	______
accomplish**ment**	______
assess**ment**	______
disappoint**ment**	______
announce**ment**	______
judge**ment**	______
arrange**ment**	______
agree**ment**	______
enrol**ment**	______
involve**ment**	______
retire**ment**	______
require**ment**	______

1 Write the list words as base word + **ment**.

investment → ______ + ment
accomplishment → ______ + ment
disappointment → ______ + ______
assessment → ______ + ______
announcement → ______ + ______
judgement → ______ + ______
arrangement → ______ + ______
agreement → ______ + ______
enrolment → ______ + ______
involvement → ______ + ______
retirement → ______ + ______
requirement → ______ + ______

2 Choose the correct word.

All the list words are

adjectives	verbs	nouns	adverbs

Most of the base words are

adjectives	verbs	nouns	adverbs

3 Add **ment.**

excite → ______
state → ______
achieve → ______
encourage → ______
manage → ______
argue → ______

Which word drops the silent **e**?

______

In general, keep the silent **e** in order to

______.

Spelling Rules! Student Book 4 (ISBN 9780655092612) © Janelle Ho, Helen Pearson

 Circle the words in which **ment** is not a suffix.

compartment	moment	cement	adornment
comment	amusement	investment	element

5 Underline the letters that make the schwa. Some words have more than one schwa.

accomplishment	entertainment	encouragement	judgement
enjoyment	government	improvement	adjustment

What sound does the vowel in the syllable **ment** make? ____________

6 The word **department** has the root word *partire*, meaning to part or divide. The following words are from the same root word. Write a sentence for each word.

depart ____

partial ____

partition ____

apartment ____

7 Write a word that ends in the suffix **ment**. In each sentence there is a word that rhymes with the base word.

Dad will finish the ________________ for my course after our stroll.

After my PE ________________ , I was less happy because I could have run faster.

Don't annoy Grandma while she's watching TV because that will ruin her

________________ .

Suzy's ________________ of the fudge is that the caramel is the best.

Have you met the ________________ for starting a fire: heat, oxygen and fuel?

I thought the half-time ________________ was insane!

Reflection

- I can do this.
- I am not sure.
- I need help.

Unit 28

Any mushroom that has white gills or has scales on the cap is inedi**ble**.

Say Listen Look Understand Remember Practise

afford**able** ______
enjoy**able** ______
renew**able** ______
agree**able** ______
forgiv**able** ______
recognis**able** ______
soci**able** ______
imposs**ible** ______
elig**ible** ______
illeg**ible** ______
ed**ible** ______
aud**ible** ______

1 Say each word. Write the number of syllables and schwas.

Word	Syllables	Schwas
affordable		
enjoyable		
renewable		
agreeable		
forgivable		
recognisable		
sociable		
impossible		
eligible		
illegible		
edible		
audible		

2 Write the list word that is from the same word family. Then write your own word.

	List word	Own word
possible	______	______
enjoy	______	______
forgive	______	______
new	______	______
society	______	______
legible	______	______
audio	______	______
cognitive	______	______

3 Add **able** or **ible**.

cap ______	remark ______	prob ______	regret ______
fashion ______	cred ______	elig ______	divis ______
port ______	compat ______	access ______	question ______

Tip

Adverbs give more information about verbs or adjectives. Adverbs usually add **ly**.
When **ly** is added to a word ending in **able** or **ible**, change **le** to **ly**.
comfortable → *comfortably* *possible* → *possibly*

4 Write the adverb of the word in brackets to complete each sentence. You will need to add **able** or **ible**, and **ly**.

Even toddlers can draw ________________ human figures. (recognise)

The little child behaved ________________ and was rewarded by her parents. (sense)

The new oranges have an ________________ sour taste that will taste best in a cake. (agree)

The furniture was designed to be used ________________ to suit the classroom activity. (flex)

Our neighbourhood store is popular because everything it sells is ________________ priced. (afford)

Tip

The words **eligible** and **illegible** are often confused.
eligible = having the necessary qualities
illegible = unable to be read (*il* + *legible*)

5 Write **eligible** or **illegible**.

As long as you submit an original story, you are ________________ for the prize. Of course, if your handwriting is ________________, your chances of winning are nil.

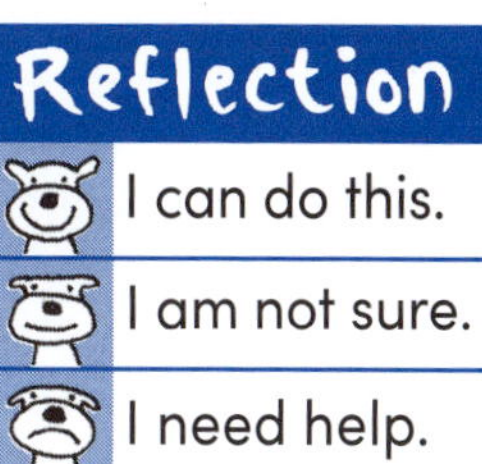

Unit 29

Australia's first computer weighed about 2 tonnes and used 3000 times more electricity than modern computers – but was around 500 000 times slower!

Say **L**isten **L**ook **U**nderstand **R**emember **P**ractise

computer	______________
laptop	______________
email	______________
internet	______________
mobile	______________
keyboard	______________
program	______________
download	______________
insert	______________
delete	______________
icon	______________
archive	______________

1 Write the list word for each picture.

______________ ______________ ______________

2 What are these symbols called?

* ______________ / ______________

______________ & ______________

3 Write the full names for these keyboard keys.

fn ______________ alt ______________

esc ______________ del ______________

Tip **Compound words** are two whole words joined together to form a new word.

soft + *ware* → *software*

4 Use a dictionary to find the meaning of *ware*.

ware = ______________________________

Write another computer compound word that ends in *ware*. ______________

5 Write the list words that are compound words.

______________ ______________ ______________

6 The same object may have different names in different countries. A mobile phone is also called a cellphone or a handphone. Use the internet to find out which countries use each word.

cellphone ______________ handphone ______________

Many terms or phrases are abbreviated to the first letter of each word.
IT = **i**nformation **t**echnology

7 Unscramble the letters to make the full name for each abbreviation.

PC aspolner pertumoc ______________________

WWW olwrd diew wbe ______________________

GB ygabgesti ______________________

USB lunarvise ariels usb ______________________

URL omufrni reecrosu rocatol ______________________

8 The names of some countries and states are commonly abbreviated. Write the full name for each abbreviation.

NZ ______________________ HK ______________________

UK ______________________ USA ______________________

NY ______________________ ACT ______________________

9 Abbreviations are sometimes used in email, text messages and on websites. Write the full text for each abbreviation.

LOL ______________________ ASAP ______________________

BTW ______________________ FAQ ______________________

10 Write the correct form of a list word to complete each sentence.

I spend time every afternoon ______________ my cousin overseas.

Grandpa is still trying to learn the ______________ on his new phone.

Our computer at home is ______________ so that Mum and Dad can check what we're using it for.

______________ big files from the internet can take a long time.

Oh no! I think I've accidentally ______________ the research I did on dolphins.

Reflection

I can do this.

I am not sure.

I need help.

Murphy the donkey was given the Purple Cross in honour of all the courage**ous** donkeys that carried wounded troops at Gallipoli.

1 Make compound words by using one word from each box.

key	lap	down	soft	bar
ware	load	board	code	top

__________ __________ __________ __________ __________

2 Write the adjective form of the word by adding **y**, **ous**, **able** or **ible**.

sag	danger	recognise	rely	courage
__________	__________	__________	__________	__________
regret	winter	fault	vary	audio
__________	__________	__________	__________	__________

3 Replace the underlined words with one word. Rewrite the sentence.

Mr Smit can't open the <u>document that I added</u> to my email.

____

Filipo hates it when we have a <u>situation when we don't get along</u>.

____

We will meet <u>people who report on the news</u> who will talk about their experiences.

____

The sewing was so professional that the stitches <u>couldn't be seen</u>.

____

The one who saves the hero at the beginning of the story turns out to be the <u>wicked person</u>.

____

 Write a word ending in **ous** to describe each character.

Pedro always wants to find out more about things. He is ________________.

Janet is feeling ________________ about having to welcome the visitor.

My dog Max gets very ________________ whenever I play with my cat.

When Lara discovered her sister had been secretly reading her emails, she was ________________.

John has appeared in many television commercials. He is now ________________.

5 Circle the word that does not make sense in each sentence. Write the correct word.

The guest was most discontinued at the poor service. ________________

I'm going to put all the documents I don't need into the chive. ________________

Don't forget to delete the address or the email can't be sent. ________________

It's incredible how eligible the plastic food looks! ________________

Kate can't swim the length of the pool so she swam the breath. As a result, she was qualified. ________________ ________________

6 Proofread this text. The text has five words that are incorrect. Circle the mistakes. Then write the correct spelling of the words in the boxes.

My parents just bought me an affordable computter. They say it is an innvestment in my future as long as I don't just use it for entertinment. I'll use it to practice being an auther.

Unit 31

Lyrebirds are excellent mimics. They can imitate the sounds of other birds, animals, people and even chainsaws, horns and trains!

Meow

Say Listen Look Understand Remember Practise

mimic ______
critic ______
exotic ______
acidic ______
dramatic ______
fantastic ______
terrific ______
tragic ______
energetic ______
automatic ______
enthusiastic ______
genetic ______

1 Write the list words in the correct group. Some words can be used more than once. Use a dictionary if you need help.

Verbs
______

Adjectives
______
______
______
______
______
______
______
______
______
______

Nouns
______
______

2 Follow the pattern to add **ic**.

base + ic → basic
mime + ___ → ______
scene + ___ → ______
automate + ___ → ______

3 Write the adjective formed from the base word.

terrify → terrific
energy → ______
giant → ______
fantasy → ______
enthusiasm → ______
magnet → ______
drama → ______
tragedy → ______

Spelling Rules! Student Book 4 (ISBN 9780655092612) © Janelle Ho, Helen Pearson

s, **ed** and **ing** are verb suffixes. When you add **ed** and **ing** to a verb ending in **ic**, add a **k**. This keeps the hard **c** sound.

picnic → picnicked, picnicking

There is no change when **s** is added.

Add the suffix to each verb.

panic + ed → ______________ panic + ing → ______________

mimic + ed → ______________ mimic + ing → ______________

Colour the right word.

Eric loves summer. He usually | picnics | picnicks | with his family in the Botanic Gardens.

When the fire alarm sounded, there was no sign of | panic | panick |. It was only when we saw a rat that we | paniced | panicked |!

Julie is a good | mimic | mimick |. She's always | mimicing | mimicking | her classmates and teachers.

Write list words.

Beau has red hair like his dad and uncles. It must be ______________.

The players haven't stopped running yet. They're certainly very ______________.

My friends aren't ______________ about learning pottery. They'd rather paint.

The way that lightning lit up the sky was most ______________.

Mowing the lawn is hard work! Wouldn't it be ______________ if someone invented an ______________ lawnmower?

Write a list word that is a synonym.

reviewer ______________ imitate ______________

lively ______________ eager ______________

unusual ______________ heartbreaking ______________

Unit 32

In winter, a snowshoe hare's fur changes from brown to white, so that predators have trouble seeing it against the snow. Now, that's a surviv**al** trick!

Say **L**isten **L**ook **U**nderstand **R**emember **P**ractise

capit**al**	___________
hospit**al**	___________
logic**al**	___________
magic**al**	___________
nation**al**	___________
natur**al**	___________
digit**al**	___________
optic**al**	___________
crimin**al**	___________
critic**al**	___________
surviv**al**	___________
emotion**al**	___________

1 Add **al** to the base word.

magic → ___________

nation → ___________

nature → ___________

survive → ___________

arrive → ___________

2 Write the base words. Use a dictionary if you need help.

logical ___________

emotional ___________

criminal ___________

personal ___________

Tip Adding **al** to a word usually changes it to an adjective. Some words ending in **al** are both nouns and adjectives.

3 Write list words that are nouns. Put an asterisk next to the ones that can also be adjectives.

___________ ___________ ___________ ___________ ___________

Choose one asterisked word. Write a sentence for each usage.

Noun: ___________

Adjective: ___________

4 Write words ending in **al**.

to do with your teeth ___________

to do with your mind ___________

to do with your eyes ___________

to do with your body ___________

to do with your spine ___________

Spelling Rules! Student Book 4 (ISBN 9780655092612) © Janelle Ho, Helen Pearson

5 Draw lines or shapes to match each label.

vertical	horizontal	diagonal	symmetrical

6 Rearrange the letters to make an **al** word that completes each sentence.

The Danish __________ (oyral) family lives in Copenhagen, the __________ (tapical) city of Denmark.

The __________ (caoll) shops hold a street market once a month.

Dogs are good pets because they are __________ (alloy).

An avatar is a __________ (glaidit) person in a computer game.

Regular __________ (cailshyp) exercise is both fun and healthy.

With the internet, we live in a __________ (bollag) village.

Tip Etymology is the study of the origins and development of words.

7 The word *final* comes from the Latin word *finis*, which means *limit* or *boundary*. Use a dictionary to find the meanings of these related words.

finish ______________________________

finite ______________________________

define ______________________________

definite ______________________________

8 Make a mnemonic to help you remember how to spell *definite*.

Reflection

- I can do this.
- I am not sure.
- I need help.

Unit 33

The average person can only memorise 7 digits. You can increase that by using an mnemonic.

Say Listen Look Understand Remember Practise

lessen	______
stiffen	______
toughen	______
sadden	______
awaken	______
straighten	______
finalise	______
memorise	______
fantasise	______
energise	______
sympathise	______
visualise	______

Tip **en** changes an adjective to a verb.

1 Write the list words as base word + **en**.

lessen → less + ______

stiffen → ______ + en

toughen → ______ + ______

sadden → ______ + ______

awaken → ______ + ______

straighten → ______ + ______

2 Add **en**. Remember to apply your spelling rules.

fast ______	short ______
light ______	shake ______
flat ______	quick ______
deaf ______	rot ______

Tip **ise** changes a noun to a verb.

3 Write the list word that is from the same word family.

final	memory	energy	visual
______	______	______	______

State the spelling rule for words ending in **y**.

______

4 Add **ise**.

fantasy ______ sympathy ______ summary ______

Spelling Rules! Student Book 4 (ISBN 9780655092612) © Janelle Ho, Helen Pearson

5 Write a list word to complete each sentence. You may need to add a suffix.

Dad found Tony ________________ the pet cat's tail.

Grandma was ________________ to learn of her friend's illness.

I love to ________________ about what it would be like to live in space.

We love where we live because we are ________________ every morning by birdsong.

Mum has an ________________ cold shower after work.

6 Answer the questions.

What is a homophone of lessen? ________________

What is an antonym of lessen? ________________

What is a synonym of lessen? ________________

What is a homophone of straight? ________________

What is an antonym of straighten? ________________

What is a synonym of straighten? ________________

7 The word *memory* comes from the Latin word *memor*, which means *mindful*. Write the meanings of these related words. Use a dictionary if you need help.

memory ________________________________

memorise ________________________________

memorial ________________________________

remember ________________________________

8 Why is it important to sympathise with others? Write a text that answers this question.

____

____

____

____

____

____

Reflection

I can do this.
I am not sure.
I need help.

An American boy once boarded a train alone and travelled 160 kilometres – in his sleep!

Say Listen Look Understand Remember Practise

travel ____________

relax ____________

journey ____________

caravan ____________

luggage ____________

budget ____________

museum ____________

attraction ____________

entertainment____________

accommodation

____

sightseeing ____________

restaurant ____________

1 Break each word up into its base word and suffix.

	base word	suffix
attraction		
entertainment		
accommodation		

2 These words can all be used in different ways. Tick boxes to show which ways they can be used.

	noun	verb	adjective
travel	☐	☐	☐
relaxing	☐	☐	☐
journey	☐	☐	☐
budget	☐	☐	☐
sightseeing	☐	☐	☐

Complete the table.

word	add s or es	add ed	add ing
relax			relaxing
journey	journeys		
budget		budgeted	
travel	travels		

Which words above are spelt differently in American English?

____________ ____________

Spelling Rules! Student Book 4 (ISBN 9780655092612) © Janelle Ho, Helen Pearson

4 Write a word that matches the definition.

_______________ suitcases and other bags

_______________ a place where things from the past are displayed

_______________ a place to eat

_______________ take a trip to another place

_______________ includes hotels, motels and caravans

_______________ what tourists do

_______________ a plan to spend money wisely

Tip

A **mnemonic** is a memory trick.
*Caravan starts with **car** and is followed by **a van**.*

5 Write or draw your own mnemonic for these words.

restaurant	luggage	accommodation

6 The city or country in which each attraction is found is hidden in each sentence. Circle the letters and write the city/country in the box.

Mr Chupar is afraid of heights and will not be climbing the Eiffel Tower.

Raja panicked when he thought he had to walk up Mount Fuji!

I could not understand our guide at the Taj Mahal because he spoke in dialect.

Sue wrote a poem about the Leaning Tower of Pisa. Her dad thought it a lyrical miracle.

Reflection

- I can do this.
- I am not sure.
- I need help.

Unit 35 Revision

The weather on the planet Neptune is seriously extreme. The wind can blow at up to 2000 km/h!

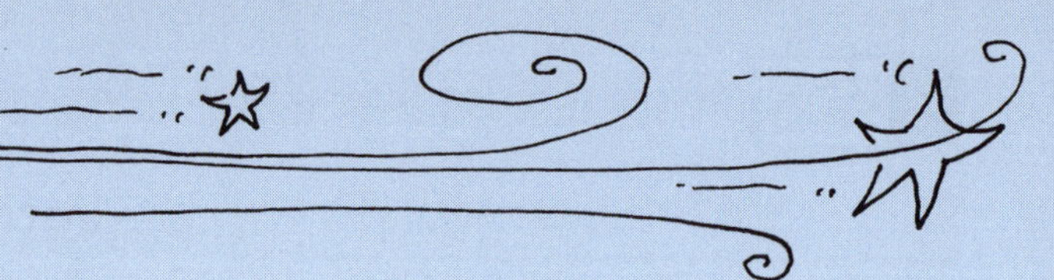

 **1** Write double consonants to complete these words.

te _ _ ific   su _ _ est   a _ _ raction   po _ _ e _ _

reco _ _ end   sa _ _ hire   a _ _ istant   exa _ _ erate

2 Complete the tables.

verb	noun
	survival
grow	
measure	
	memory
	breath
locate	
fail	
	explosion

adjective	noun
agreeable	
	guilt
courageous	
energetic	
strong	
clean	
	fantasy
	envy

 **3** Write a synonym for each word. (Clue: Each synonym has an **er** sound, although the spelling might be different.)

happen ______   diary ______   outing ______

fantastic ______   sure ______   manners ______

4 Write an antonym for each word. (Clue: Each antonym has five letters.)

last ______   end ______   tight ______

light ______   approximate ______   small ______

 **5** Form antonyms by adding a prefix to each word.

____formal   ____honest   ____legal   ____contented   ____decisive

____advantage   ____complete   ____pleasant   ____behave   ____logical

6 Write a more interesting word for the underlined word or words.

Kerry <u>looked</u> everywhere for the earring she lost. ____________

I was <u>happy</u> that we won the match. ____________

Fawaz was surprised when a kangaroo suddenly <u>came out</u>. ____________

Sam was <u>very tired</u> after the cross-country carnival. ____________

7 These words are sometimes confused. Colour the correct word.

The dog escaped because the [not | knot] had come [lose | loose].

I [wander | wonder] [were | where] I can hide Mum's present.

Mum is [vain | vein] and covers the [vain | vein] on her face with make-up.

Do you know what the [affect | effect] of adding vinegar to corn flour is?

I have [accepted | excepted] the invitation, so I'll go [weather | whether] or not it rains.

No, you're not [eligible | illegible] for the prize. In fact, because you are the president's child, it would be [illegible | illegal] to award it to you.

8 Replace the name of the author with a real word. The title gives you a clue. The first one has been done for you. Hint! Say the author's name aloud.

Spices by Flay Ver <u>flavour</u>

Sweet Treats by Dee Zirt ____________

A day at the museum by X. Kershen ____________

Fool the cops by V. Len ____________

Surviving the news by Gern Elist ____________

Taking a tumble by Jim Nay C. Em ____________

No need to be afraid by Fo Beer ____________

The best places to eat by Rez Traunt ____________

Hearing aids by Or D. Bul ____________

What to wear in the desert by Car Key ____________

Joining words by Kon Junk Shun ____________

LIST WORDS IN UNIT ORDER

Unit 1
oppose
endure
revise
complete
arrange
escape
persuade
realise
collide
assume
include
declare

Unit 2
copy
hurry
guilty
mystery
variety
deny
apply
simplify
qualify
display
prey
annoy

Unit 3
begin
forget
regret
occur
prefer
enter
offer
answer
visit
happen
target
label
detail

Unit 4
engulf
behalf
cough
trough
phase
phobia
phantom
metaphor
emphasise
biography
amphibian
sophisticated

Unit 5
odd
stiff
err
recall
install
swell
thrill
floss
discuss
possess
witness
embarrass

Unit 7
least
eager
release
dread
ahead
heavy
health
meant
instead
pleasant
jealous
weather

Unit 8
ginger
gently
general
average
generous
religion
intelligent
fragile
generation
advantage
emergency
gymnasium

Unit 9
bandage
sponge
surge
stranger
siege
badger
pledge
reject
injection
adjust
conjunction
adjective

Unit 10
niece
belief
achieve
alien
receipt
deceive
protein
weird
reign
seize
beige
feisty

Unit 11
lose
loose
breath
breathe
desert
dessert
practise
practice
wonder
wander
stationery
stationary

Unit 13
narrow
sorrow
tomorrow
loan
poach
coward
foul
announce
voucher
boundary
council
knowledge

Unit 14
verse
superb
alert
convert
deserve
determined
certain
permanent
earthquake
research
earnest
rehearsal

Unit 15
worthy
senior
surprise
further
burden
survive
journal
flavour
labour
courtesy
honour
harbour

Unit 16
nature
future
capture
failure
creature
feature
measure
pleasure
leisure
adventure
furniture
temperature

Unit 17
ruby
scarlet
lilac
violet
emerald
indigo
crimson
azure
khaki
ochre
turquoise
sapphire

Unit 19
exist
exchange
examination
explosion
expensive
exaggerate
excursion
exceed
except
extinct
exhausted
exhibition

Unit 20
unfamiliar
undeveloped
unbroken
unquestioning
inactive
incomplete
informal
invisible
disease

disqualify
discontented
discontinue

Unit 21

rejection
suggestion
location
separation
confusion
decision
conclusion
greatness
selfishness
stubbornness
cleanliness
forgetfulness

Unit 22

fourth
fifth
eighth
ninth
twelfth
growth
warmth
length
strength
width
depth
breadth

Unit 23

accept
appeal
stubborn
villain
pollute
approach
opportunity
attitude
necessary
recommend
occasion
aggressive

Unit 25

author
grocer
carpenter
lawyer
assistant
accountant
electrician
politician
journalist
pharmacist
chef
pilot

Unit 26

serious
precious
delicious
famous
nervous
dangerous
courageous
furious
cautious
envious
spacious
various

Unit 27

investment
accomplishment
assessment
disappointment
announcement
judgement
arrangement
agreement
enrolment
involvement
retirement
requirement

Unit 28

affordable
enjoyable
renewable
agreeable
forgivable
recognisable
sociable
impossible
eligible
illegible
edible
audible

Unit 29

computer
laptop
email
internet
mobile
keyboard
program
download
insert
delete
icon
archive

Unit 31

mimic
critic
exotic
acidic
dramatic
fantastic
terrific
tragic
energetic
automatic
enthusiastic
genetic

Unit 32

capital
hospital
logical
magical
national
natural
digital
optical
criminal
critical
survival
emotional

Unit 33

lessen
stiffen
toughen
sadden
awaken
straighten
finalise
memorise
fantasise
energise
sympathise
visualise

Unit 34

travel
relax
journey
caravan
luggage
budget
museum
attraction
entertainment
accommodation
sightseeing
restaurant

List words in alphabetical order

Word	Unit
accept	Unit 23
accommodation	Unit 34
accomplishment	Unit 27
accountant	Unit 25
achieve	Unit 10
acidic	Unit 31
adjective	Unit 9
adjust	Unit 9
advantage	Unit 8
adventure	Unit 16
affordable	Unit 28
aggressive	Unit 23
agreeable	Unit 28
agreement	Unit 27
ahead	Unit 7
alert	Unit 14
alien	Unit 10
amphibian	Unit 4
announce	Unit 13
announcement	Unit 27
annoy	Unit 2
appeal	Unit 23
apply	Unit 2
approach	Unit 23
archive	Unit 29
arrange	Unit 1
arrangement	Unit 27
assessment	Unit 27
assistant	Unit 25
assume	Unit 1
attitude	Unit 23
attraction	Unit 34
audible	Unit 28
author	Unit 25
automatic	Unit 31
average	Unit 8
awaken	Unit 33
azure	Unit 17
badger	Unit 9
bandage	Unit 9
begin	Unit 3
behalf	Unit 4
beige	Unit 10
belief	Unit 10
biography	Unit 4
boundary	Unit 13
breadth	Unit 22
breath	Unit 11
breathe	Unit 11
budget	Unit 34
burden	Unit 15
capital	Unit 32
capture	Unit 16
caravan	Unit 34
carpenter	Unit 25
cautious	Unit 26
certain	Unit 14
chef	Unit 25
cleanliness	Unit 21
collide	Unit 1
complete	Unit 1
computer	Unit 29
conclusion	Unit 21
confusion	Unit 21
conjunction	Unit 9
convert	Unit 14
copy	Unit 2
cough	Unit 4
council	Unit 13
courageous	Unit 26
courtesy	Unit 15
coward	Unit 13
creature	Unit 16
criminal	Unit 32
crimson	Unit 17
critic	Unit 31
critical	Unit 32
dangerous	Unit 26
deceive	Unit 10
decision	Unit 21
declare	Unit 1
delete	Unit 29
delicious	Unit 26
deny	Unit 2
depth	Unit 22
desert	Unit 11
deserve	Unit 14
dessert	Unit 11
detail	Unit 3
determined	Unit 14
digital	Unit 32
disappointment	Unit 27
display	Unit 2
discontented	Unit 20
discontinue	Unit 20
discuss	Unit 5
disease	Unit 20
disqualify	Unit 20
download	Unit 29
dramatic	Unit 31
dread	Unit 7
eager	Unit 7
earnest	Unit 14
earthquake	Unit 14
edible	Unit 28
eighth	Unit 22
electrician	Unit 25
eligible	Unit 28
email	Unit 29
embarrass	Unit 5
emerald	Unit 17
emergency	Unit 8
emotional	Unit 32
emphasise	Unit 4
endure	Unit 1
energetic	Unit 31
energise	Unit 33
engulf	Unit 4
enjoyable	Unit 28
enrolment	Unit 27
enter	Unit 3
entertainment	Unit 34
enthusiastic	Unit 31
envious	Unit 26
err	Unit 5
escape	Unit 1
exaggerate	Unit 19
examination	Unit 19
exceed	Unit 19
except	Unit 19
exchange	Unit 19
excursion	Unit 19
exhausted	Unit 19
exhibition	Unit 19
exist	Unit 19
exotic	Unit 31
expensive	Unit 19
explosion	Unit 19
extinct	Unit 19
failure	Unit 16
famous	Unit 26
fantasise	Unit 33
fantastic	Unit 31
feature	Unit 16
feisty	Unit 10
fifth	Unit 22
finalise	Unit 33
flavour	Unit 15
floss	Unit 5
forget	Unit 3
forgetfulness	Unit 21
forgivable	Unit 28
foul	Unit 13
fourth	Unit 22
fragile	Unit 8
furious	Unit 26
furniture	Unit 16
further	Unit 15
future	Unit 16
general	Unit 8
generation	Unit 8
generous	Unit 8
genetic	Unit 31
gently	Unit 8
ginger	Unit 8
greatness	Unit 21
grocer	Unit 25
growth	Unit 22
guilty	Unit 2
gymnasium	Unit 8
happen	Unit 3
harbour	Unit 15
health	Unit 7
heavy	Unit 7
honour	Unit 15
hospital	Unit 32
hurry	Unit 2
icon	Unit 29
illegible	Unit 28
impossible	Unit 28

Spelling Rules! Student Book 4 (ISBN 9780655092612) © Janelle Ho, Helen Pearson

SPELLING RULES AND TIPS

Adding **es**, **ed** and **ing**

If a word ends in silent **e**, drop the **e** before adding the suffixes **ed** or **ing**.

smile → smiled *ride → riding*

If a word ends in **y**, change **y** to **i** before adding **es** or **ed**.

try → tries *spy → spied*

But keep the **y** when adding **ing**.

try → trying

If a verb ends in **ic**, when you add **ed** or **ing** add a **k** to keep the hard **c** sound.

mimic → mimicked, mimicking

But the verb stays the same when **s** is added.

mimic → mimics

Adding **y**

If a word has a single vowel followed by a single consonant, double the consonant before adding **y**.

mud → muddy

If a word ends in silent **e**, drop the **e** before adding **y**.

juice → juicy

Adding **ous**

If the base word ends in silent **e**, drop the **e** before adding **ous**.

fame → famous

If the base word ends in **ce**, change the **e** to **i** before adding **ous**.

space → spacious

If the base word ends in **ge**, keep the **e** when adding **ous**.

courage → courageous

If the base word ends in **y**, change **y** to **i** before adding **ous**.

envy → envious

Adding **ion**

Some verbs can be changed into nouns by adding **ion**.

act → action

If the verb ends in silent **e**, drop the **e** before adding **ion**.

create → creation

If the verb ends in **de**, change **de** to **s** before adding **ion**.

divide → division

Spelling Rules! Student Book 4 (ISBN 9780655092612) © Janelle Ho, Helen Pearson